STARTER SOURDOUGH

Starter SOURDOUGH

The *Step-by-Step* Guide to
SOURDOUGH STARTERS
Baking Loaves, Baguettes, Pancakes, and More

Carroll Pellegrinelli

callisto
publishing
an imprint of Sourcebooks

I dedicate this book to my husband, Mark, and daughter, Loretta, who have always offered unconditional love and support.

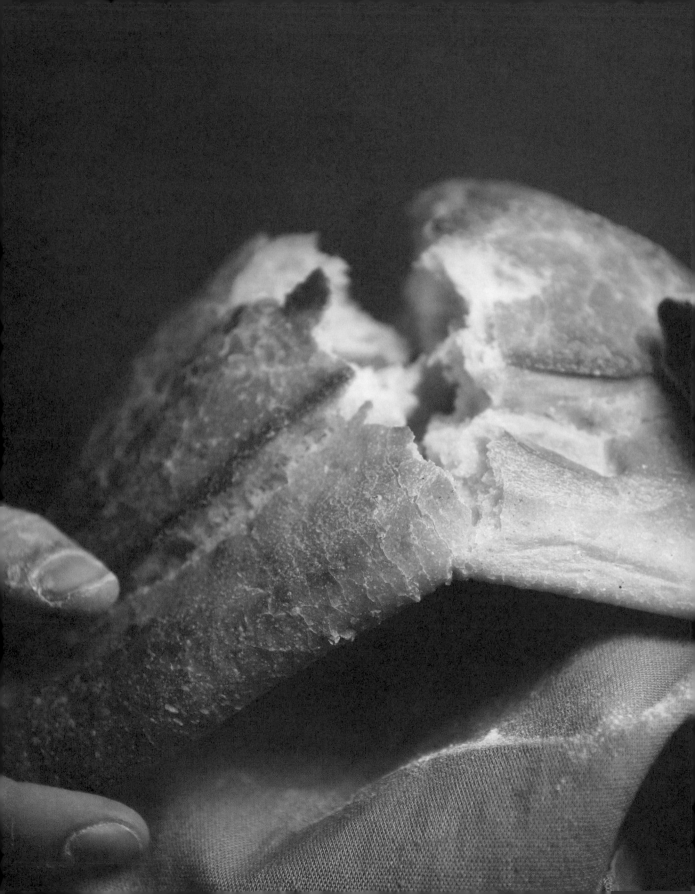

CONTENTS

INTRODUCTION
THE SENTIMENTALITY, SCIENCE, AND SUPERIORITY OF SOURDOUGH

Hello, my name is Carroll and I have a confession to make . . . I love to bake. The joy of baking was instilled in me at an early age by my parents. By the time I could reach the counter, my eager little hands were creaming butter and sugars. Making and baking desserts was my mother's specialty. And, although he didn't start baking bread until I was in high school, my father would soon also teach me the joys of bread baking, which became his way to alleviate daily frustrations. Kneading dough is perfect for that purpose. Each time you punch the dough and slap it on your work surface, you can feel the aggression leave your body. Once the calm sets in, it's time to gently shape the dough.

Baking bread was an on and off activity for me until my husband was diagnosed with type 2 diabetes—at which point I stopped baking bread. My father's old breadboard was stored away, and the bread machine was sold at a yard sale. In hindsight, giving up bread baking was a mistake. My husband continued to eat bread, even though it was in moderation. Had I known that using a sourdough starter was the best choice of bread for a type 2 diabetic, I would never have stopped.

Combining flour, which contains wild yeast, with pure filtered or bottled water in a warm environment is how the fermentation process begins. The fermentation in the sourdough starter helps process the bread so when it goes into the body it lessens the sugar spike. Naturally, each individual may experience it differently. The sourdough starter can be used in almost any recipe that involves flour. Every time you use your own sourdough starter you put a personal stamp on that baked good. No one else in the world will make that bread or baked good just like you because they aren't using your own special sourdough starter.

How good is homemade sourdough bread? It contains fewer man-made chemicals, and the sourdough starter is made with only two—yes two—ingredients: flour and water, plus the air we breathe. You can't get much simpler than that. Sourdough is not hard to make, it's just time consuming. That's the hardest part. For example, if you decide to bake a loaf of sourdough bread on Sunday, you will have to know when to start planning to make that loaf. If you are lucky enough to bake every day or every weekend, time management will be easy.

Let's start by making your own personal sourdough starter. Once you've made it, taken care of it, fed and nurtured it, you'll be able to make your very first loaf of sourdough bread. It is only the beginning. Before you know it, you'll be adding your very own personal sourdough starter to everything that has flour in it. No store or bakery can replace the smells and tastes of your own personal bread baking.

I hope you enjoy my book. It's filled with everything you should know about sourdough starter and all of the wonderful recipes you can make with it.

Remember, any recipe that uses flour can be adapted with the addition of your own personal, made-with-love, sourdough starter.

PART ONE
Your Starter

Sourdough starter is the be-all and end-all of bread baking. It is that spark that makes breads and other baked goods stand out on their own. No two starters are the same and neither are the baked goods that are made with them.

Chapter One
START WITH YOUR STARTER

Sourdough starters have existed for centuries, and they aren't just the province of professional bakers. The early Egyptians used sourdough starters to make breads. Today there are families all over the world that have maintained sourdough starters for generations.

A sourdough starter is created by fermenting a mixture of flour and water. The wild yeast found in the flour, combined with the good bacteria that develops during the fermentation process, causes the gas CO_2, carbon dioxide, to release. This reaction, which may take up to a week, is what bakers look for when they add sourdough starter to their bread dough. The gas bubbles help develop the holes inside each loaf of bread.

Anyone can create and maintain a sourdough starter. It's not difficult. A healthy long-lasting starter is maintained by a regular feeding schedule of flour and water. The feedings may occur from a couple times a day to once a week. The starter is ready when a teaspoon of it floats in a glass of water.

Why the Starter?

The moment you create your sourdough starter is the moment your breads truly are your own. They will be unique. No one else will be able to reproduce them exactly because you made them with your own personal starter.

By maintaining your sourdough starter you can make not only the most delightful breads, but also other tasty baked goods, such as cakes, cookies, and pastries.

Bread and other baked goods made with a sourdough starter have a longer shelf life because the starter is its own culture of microbes made from good bacteria, which fight off bad bacteria, which, in turn, fight off mold.

A sourdough starter is versatile. Feel free to change the starter by using different flours and grains. Just be sure to save some of the original starter so it lives on in case your later starters fail. You can have several differently flavored starters going at one time—they just all have to be fed regularly to survive.

If you bake only occasionally, your sourdough starter may be frozen or dried (see page 15 for complete drying instructions). Freezing sourdough isn't much different than refrigerating it. The only difference is that frozen sourdough starter doesn't have to be fed. To freeze the starter, begin with 9½ ounces (1 cup) of active, recently fed (within the last 6 to 12 hours) sourdough starter. When you're ready to bake bread, remove the sourdough starter from the freezer and let it defrost on the counter. Once defrosted, begin its regular feeding schedule again. When you see the starter bubbling and growing (from three days to one week), you know it's time to make bread.

The Simple Sourdough Starter Recipe

You can't get simpler than a sourdough starter made with only three ingredients: whole-wheat flour, pure filtered or bottled water, and unbleached bread flour. Some starter recipes may call for packaged dry yeast, but sourdough purists prefer all-natural wild yeast, even though it increases the number of days until the starter can be used to bake bread. The addition of instant or active yeast speeds up the process.

Some starter recipes may also include salt, which is typically used for preservation and flavor, but in the recipe here, fermentation acts as a natural form of preservation, making additional preservation ingredients unnecessary. The best time to add flavor is by adding salt when the starter is mixed with other ingredients to make the bread dough.

When making your starter, be sure to weigh the flour instead of using a dry measuring cup. A successful starter is made with equally weighted ingredients. One cup of flour doesn't weigh the same as 1 cup of water, and 1 cup of flour, measured by different people using differing methods, won't weigh the same either.

Starter Ingredients

This starter could be the beginning of several years of homemade baked goods. Be sure to use the required ingredients, in exact weighted amounts and temperatures, and you won't be disappointed. You should end up with about 2 cups of starter, plus some extra.

4 ounces (1 cup) 100 percent whole-grain whole-wheat flour Wild yeast and microorganisms make whole-grain whole-wheat flour the best flour to use for sourdough starter. It provides a strong base to continue to build the starter. It is possible to make the entire starter with this flour, but it doesn't maintain the desired results of a long-lasting starter. It may become too heavy with an overpowering sour smell.

4 ounces (½ cup) pure filtered or bottled water Pure filtered or bottled water is used because tap water has chlorine. If you use filtered water from your refrigerator, heat it to at least lukewarm (90°F to 100°F). Cold water will lengthen the time it takes the starter to activate. I keep water at room temperature (75°F) to use in breads. If it's not warm enough, I hold the sealed bottom of the water bottle under hot running water for a few minutes and that seems to bring the temperature up high enough. Another way to heat it is to pour the water into a measuring cup and carefully bring it to the desired temperature in the microwave, heating in 10-second intervals.

4 ounces (scant 1 cup) unbleached bread flour Unbleached bread flour is used to feed the starter. By choosing this flour as the food for the starter, there won't be an overwhelming whole-wheat taste or texture. Bread flour also adds more protein, such as gluten, to the bread, making it sturdier.

Ingredients That Boost Natural Fermentation

The fermentation process begins when the wild yeast from flour and the environment combine with pure filtered or bottled water in a lightly covered container. Regular feedings of additional flour and water aid the process. Using water that is warmer, but not too warm, will increase the rate of fermentation. To enhance or speed this process, other ingredients may be added. Yeast feeds on sugar, but only if the sugar is added in small amounts. Salt added in even smaller amounts may also aid fermentation. Some people swear by using pineapple juice just in the beginning of making the starter. The best way to boost fermentation is by increasing the temperature of the starter. Keeping the starter in an oven with just the light on will accomplish this. Be very careful. It is just as easy to kill a starter with too much heat as it is to boost the process.

Starter Step-by-Step

Anyone can make a healthy sourdough starter, but developing and maintaining it requires *regular feedings*. Use a written, phone, or computer calendar to keep track of the feeding schedule. When establishing the starter, **weigh the flour and water in ounces** to get a more accurate measurement than in cups (volume). Even using this recipe, not all starters will come out the same. Sourdough starters made with wild yeast will vary from one location to the next, affecting their weight.

Day 1

In a 4-quart glass or plastic container, combine 4 ounces (1 cup) whole-wheat flour and 4 ounces (½ cup) lukewarm (90°F to 100°F) pure filtered or bottled water. Stir until the mixture is completely combined. Loosely cover the container. If using a glass bowl, just cover the top with a clean kitchen towel. If using a plastic container, lightly set the lid on top. Place the container in a warm, draft-free place. In the winter, use the oven with the light on. To avoid any mishaps, place a note over the Bake button as a reminder not to turn the oven on.

> **Note:** Do not use metal or stainless steel bowls for sourdough starter storage. The fermentation necessary in the starter is an acidic reaction and the acid will eat through even the toughest metals. The metal will become discolored and the starter will end up with an undesirable metallic taste.

Day 2
24 HOURS LATER

There isn't much change in the starter except, perhaps, for the appearance of a few bubbles around the edges and across the top. Feed the starter with 4 ounces (scant 1 cup) unbleached bread flour and 4 ounces (½ cup) lukewarm (90°F to 100°F) pure filtered or bottled water. Stir for a minute or two to incorporate the flour and water. Once combined, stir a few more times to get a bit of air into the starter. Loosely cover your container and place it where it was originally stored.

Day 3
24 HOURS LATER

A few more bubbles may have appeared, and the smell may be getting a little sour. Stir in another 4 ounces (scant 1 cup) unbleached bread flour and 4 ounces (½ cup) lukewarm (90°F to 100°F) pure filtered or bottled water. Stir together a little bit longer to incorporate more air. Re-cover your container for storage.

Day 4
24 HOURS LATER

Today you should see a large increase in volume (about 50 percent, depending on room temperature, etc.), and notice that the sour/fruity smell is more pronounced. Feed the starter once again with 4 ounces (scant 1 cup) unbleached bread flour and 4 ounces (½ cup) lukewarm (90°F to 100°F) pure filtered or bottled water. Stir until everything is completely incorporated. Re-cover your container for storage.

Day 5
24 HOURS LATER

The starter is ready to use if it has a healthy sour smell, contains lots of bubbles, looks spongy, and has increased in volume by about another 25 to 50 percent. Feed it one more time with 4 ounces (scant 1 cup) unbleached bread flour and 4 ounces (½ cup) lukewarm (90°F to 100°F) pure filtered or bottled water. Stir the starter. Let it rest for at least 6 hours. Remove 9½ ounces (1 cup) for use in a recipe. Remove another 9½ ounces (1 cup) to refrigerate in a sealed glass or plastic container for later use. Throw away any remaining starter or use it in the recipes in chapter 4.

Once-a-Week Feedings

Remove half the starter from the refrigerator (use it in any recipe in chapter 4 or give it to a friend). Feed the remaining starter with 4 ounces (scant 1 cup) unbleached bread flour and 4 ounces (½ cup) lukewarm (90°F to 100°F) pure filtered or bottled water. Leave the fed starter out, loosely covered, for a couple of hours and then return it to the refrigerator, tightly covered.

Baking with Refrigerated Starter

Remove the starter from the refrigerator at least 24 hours before using it. Be sure to feed it once again with 4 ounces (scant 1 cup) unbleached bread flour, or follow the recipe directions and use the type of flour required, and 4 ounces (½ cup) luke-warm (90°F to 100°F) pure filtered or bottled water. The starter is ready for baking 6 to 12 hours after the feeding. Cover the remaining starter and place it back into the refrigerator.

Can This Starter Be Saved? What is the difference between a good starter and a bad one? A good starter has a sour smell and is light brown in color with lots of bubbles. A bad starter smells sour and sweetly rancid, like the bottom of a trash can. The look is typically darker with other colors appearing, such as yellow and red. There is no reason to try to save a bad starter when a new one begins with only flour and water.

Starters Using Whole Grains and Other Flours

The best starters begin with a whole-grain flour. Whole-grain flours are full of wild yeast. Between the wild yeast and the fermentation achieved through the starter process, you will produce a longer lasting, healthy bread.

The Simple Sourdough Starter Recipe (page 4) can be adapted to use other grains. The change is accomplished via the sourdough starter maintenance process. Instead of feeding the starter with the unbleached bread flour, use one or more of the many choices following. Be sure to save 9½ ounces (1 cup) of the original starter, just in case you don't care for the modified starter. To seal the deal, use the same flour used for feeding when making the bread dough. Feel free to create a combination such as a rye starter along with pumpernickel added to the bread dough.

Flaxseed Flour

Typically, flaxseed flour is not used as a starter ingredient. It is better used with the established sourdough starter. For best results, soak the flaxseed before adding it to the bread dough, otherwise it will absorb the necessary liquid in the bread. Flaxseed is a good source of fiber and omega-3 essential fatty acids.

Pumpernickel Flour

Also known as dark rye flour, this flour adds an even deeper level of sour, or earthiness, to a sourdough starter. Combining light rye flour with pumpernickel is how marble rye is made.

Rye Flour

Rye is considered one of the best flours to use when making a sourdough starter. There are three types of rye: light, medium, and dark. The grains in rye flour are left whole during processing. This means more nutrients are left in the grain. Rye flour alone imparts its own sourness to the bread.

Semolina, a.k.a. Durum Flour

Although semolina has a higher protein and gluten content, it doesn't make a good bread dough. It is often used to keep bread doughs from sticking to baking dishes and baking stones. It is a yellow-orange, crunchy grain frequently found on the top or bottom of baked breads.

Soy Flour

Besides being a natural source of dietary fiber, soy offers a tremendous source of vegetable protein. No more than 30 to 40 percent of wheat flour should be replaced by soy flour. If more is used, the bread will be very dense and not rise as desired.

Spelt Flour

A nutty, slightly sweet flavor typifies this flour made from an ancient grain. Of the flours in this list, spelt can be successfully used to begin a starter. It doesn't have as much gluten as whole-wheat flour. It will still make a good loaf of bread, although the bread may not rise as high or be as light as other breads.

Whole-Wheat Flour

This flour is heavier and higher in fiber and nutrition than all-purpose flour. The whole-wheat flour doesn't impart any additional flavor to the bread, which makes it a solid choice for beginning the starter. The interest in ancient whole-wheat flours, such as einkorn, is making them very popular choices.

Keeping Your Starter Happy and Healthy

You've made the personal commitment to create a sourdough starter like generations before you have. Don't take it lightly. A sourdough starter will—almost—become a member of the family. Treat it as such. A happy and healthy sourdough starter requires a safe place, constant care, and regular nourishment. Only a happy and healthy starter will produce tasty breads and rolls, to say nothing of the variety of other baked items limited only by your imagination.

Storing Your Starter

A healthy sourdough starter should be stored in a glass or plastic container. In the beginning, your container should be able to hold 4 quarts. Once past the original starter creation, a container no smaller than a 1-quart canning jar can be used. If you're leaving your starter out on the kitchen counter in the beginning stages, or for a 6- to 12-hour feeding, it should be in a warm place, lightly covered. If you're planning to bake with it once a week, keep it refrigerated, tightly covered.

Feeding Your Starter

Regular feeding is necessary to keep your starter healthy. If the starter is kept on the counter and is in a strong growing stage, it's fed once or twice a day. If you're storing your starter in the refrigerator, a once-a-week feeding is necessary. Write your feeding times on a calendar or use your phone for reminders.

What Kind of Flour?

The *initial feeding* in this starter recipe calls for *whole-grain whole-wheat flour*. Subsequent feedings are made with unbleached bread flour. Bread flour has more gluten—a protein that makes bread sturdier. After the initial starter is made and it's on a regular feeding schedule you can switch out the flours you feed it with. You could convert your starter from a white/wheat starter to a whole-wheat starter, a rye starter, a spelt starter, etc. The options are limited only by the types of wheat flours available to you.

How Much Flour and Water?

In the beginning, the best combination of flour and water is one in equal amounts, thus making it a 100 percent hydration starter (see page 14). The equal measurements are done **in weight,** not volume. Using a digital scale is the easiest—and most accurate—way to do it, but, while preferred, it is not absolutely necessary.

Our recipe calls for 4 ounces of water and 4 ounces of flour for the regular daily feedings. Using your liquid ingredients glass measuring cup, measure ½ cup (4 ounces) of water. Use your dry measuring cups to measure out a scant 1 cup (4 ounces) of unbleached bread flour. Note 1 cup of all-purpose flour weighs 4¼ ounces.

Is Your Starter Ready?

By Day 5, the starter should be ready. It should have a healthy sour smell, have increased in size, and have lots of bubbles. What if it doesn't? Then feed it again and check back in 24 hours. There's nothing to worry about. It'll be fine. Be patient; some starters are ready in their own time.

Sample Weekly Starter Feeding Schedule

DAY 1

NOTE THE TIME YOU DO THIS FIRST FEEDING

Combine 4 ounces (1 cup) whole-grain whole-wheat flour with 4 ounces (½ cup) lukewarm (90°F to 100°F) pure filtered or bottled water.

DAY 2

SAME TIME AS PREVIOUS DAY

Feed the starter with 4 ounces (scant 1 cup) unbleached bread flour and 4 ounces (½ cup) lukewarm (90°F to 100°F) pure filtered or bottled water.

DAY 3

SAME TIME

Feed the starter with 4 ounces (scant 1 cup) unbleached bread flour and 4 ounces (½ cup) lukewarm (90°F to 100°F) pure filtered or bottled water.

DAY 4

SAME TIME

Feed the starter with 4 ounces (scant 1 cup) unbleached bread flour and 4 ounces (½ cup) lukewarm (90°F to 100°F) pure filtered or bottled water.

DAY 5

SAME TIME

Feed the starter with 4 ounces (scant 1 cup) unbleached bread flour and 4 ounces (½ cup) lukewarm (90°F to 100°F) pure filtered or bottled water.

DAY 5+

SAME DAY, 6 HOURS LATER

Remove 9½ ounces (1 cup) starter to use in a recipe. Transfer 9½ ounces (1 cup) to a clean glass jar to refrigerate for later use. Be sure to feed it weekly.

Author's Note:
I use the calendar in my phone set with alerts to help maintain my starter. Refrigerator magnets and paper work, too.

What Is Sourdough Hydration?

Sourdough hydration is the balance between the amount of flour and water used in the starter. For a starter to be considered high hydration there must be at least 70 percent or more water than flour. Breads made with higher hydration may take longer to bake and need more proofing time. These breads also have bigger holes, and are often considered rustic or artisan due to the better development of the yeast. A starter made with less than 60 percent water is denser, with a more pronounced sour taste. Most recipes usually call for a starter made with 100 percent hydration.

How to Achieve 100 Percent Hydration

The simplest way to achieve 100 percent hydration is to begin your starter and continually feed it with equal parts flour and water. The Simple Sourdough Starter Recipe (page 4) calls for 4 ounces of flour and 4 ounces of water. Using a digital food scale is the best way to successfully make and maintain these measurements. Remember the flour and water are **measured by weight**, not volume. Measuring by volume doesn't work in 100 percent hydration because the flour and water don't weigh the same when measured in volume: 1 cup of flour weighs about 4 ounces (depending on the type) whereas 1 cup of water weighs 8 ounces.

The high hydration does make the dough difficult to knead. It may be easier to use the dough folding method (see page 24) to achieve the same effect as traditional kneading.

Working with Lower Hydration

The stiffer, lower hydration sourdough starter is often used to make items such as piecrusts, pretzels, bagels, and other things not expected to rise. Frequent kneading is necessary using doughs made with lower hydration to build the gluten. It is not uncommon for a recipe made with a stiff starter to require the addition of yeast to increase the rise.

Drying and Reactivating the Sourdough Starter

You've invested your time and mental energy into nurturing this ode to deliciousness, but what happens when you can't continue to maintain it? You don't want to lose it—but what if work is keeping you away or you want to go on vacation? Who will manage your sourdough starter's upkeep? Have out-of-town friends asked you to share your starter? How do you get it to them? There is one easy answer to all these questions: *dehydration*. Don't worry, it is simpler to accomplish than you think.

Drying Step-by-Step
STEP 1: FEED THE STARTER

Early in the day, feed 4¾ ounces (½ cup) of starter with 4 ounces (1 cup) of flour along with 4 ounces (½ cup) of lukewarm (90°F to 100°F) pure filtered or bottled water. Mix thoroughly. Loosely cover the container and put it in its normal (warm, draft-free) resting place. Depending on the kitchen and the starter's resting place, it should be bubbling nicely by afternoon. If it isn't, let it rest a little longer.

STEP 2: DRY THE STARTER

Lay two pieces of parchment paper, the size of baking sheets, on a flat surface. Divide at least 9½ ounces (1 cup), or all, of the starter, depending on how much you want to dry, between the parchment sheets. Use a rubber or metal spatula, a dough scraper, or a pastry brush to spread out the starter as thinly as possible. The thinner the layer, the quicker it will dry. Turn on the interior oven light. Carefully place the starter-covered sheets on separate racks in the oven. Depending on the humidity, the kitchen temperature, and the oven temperature, dehydration may take half a day or a couple of days. Leave the starter there until it is completely dry.

STEP 3: HANDLING THE BRITTLE STARTER

Remove the dried starter from the oven. It should almost peel off the paper in whole pieces. Add the dried pieces of starter to a resealable plastic bag. Don't overfill the bag before sealing it. Once sealed, crush the starter with your hands or a rolling pin. It is fine if the pieces end up the size of small flakes. This is where you decide what to do with the flakes. They should be stored in an airtight container either in the freezer or in a dark, cool, dry place for later use. If kept properly, the starter can be stored indefinitely. For gifts, divide the starter by putting 2 teaspoons of dried starter into 2-quart glass canning jars. Along with the jar and any recipe instructions, give your friends enough flour and bottled water to successfully begin the sourdough starter process (see page 4).

Reactivating the Dry Sourdough Starter
DAY 1: BEGIN THE REACTIVATION PROCESS

In a 2-quart glass or plastic container combine 2 teaspoons of dried sourdough starter and 2½ ounces (⅓ cup) of lukewarm (90°F to 100°F) pure filtered or bottled water. Stir and let the flakes sit for a few hours.

At the 2-hour mark check to see if the flakes have dissolved. If necessary, let them sit a bit longer.

Once completely dissolved, add 2 ounces (½ cup) of unbleached white all-purpose flour to the container and stir. Cover the container loosely. Let the sourdough starter rest in the oven with the light on for 24 hours. Stir the mixture two or three times during this time period.

DAY 2: SECOND FEEDING

Completely stir in another 1 ounce (2 tablespoons) of lukewarm (90°F to 100°F) pure filtered or bottled water and 1 ounce (scant ¼ cup) of unbleached white all-purpose flour. Check the sourdough starter in 12 hours for active bubbling. If the culture is not as bubbly as it should be, repeat this step. If it is at a good place in reactivation, continue on to the next day's schedule.

DAY 3: BACK TO THE REGULAR FEEDING SCHEDULE

Twelve hours after the last feeding, discard all but 4¾ ounces (½ cup) of the starter. Completely stir in 4 ounces (½ cup) of lukewarm (90°F to 100°F) pure filtered or bottled water and 4 ounces (1 cup) of flour. Repeat this step every 24 hours to maintain a healthy sourdough starter, or refrigerate the starter and maintain it with weekly feedings (use your discarded sourdough starter in some of the recipes in chapter 4).

Chapter Two

PREPARING YOUR KITCHEN FOR YOUR FIRST BAKE

Your sourdough starter is ready, but are you? Do you have everything you need to make that first loaf of bread, including ingredients? Make sure you have good quality butter on hand. Have you scheduled time for kneading, proofing, resting, and baking? When planning, I work backward—I want the bread at this time, which means baking has to start at this time; the final rise has to begin at this time, etc. Other times to plan for include punching down the dough, kneading, resting, and proofing, all the way back to the final feed of the starter.

A Starter Kitchen

Most likely you already possess the basic items needed for baking that first loaf of sourdough bread. If you don't have them, they are easily found online or in stores. On a budget? Local thrift stores and yard sales are full of kitchen items. Another way to get started is to borrow what you need until you've decided to become a lifelong sourdough baker. Who wouldn't lend you a pan or two if it was returned with a loaf of freshly baked sourdough bread? Following is a simple checklist to start.

o **Baking pans:** Since sourdough uses steam during the beginning of its baking process, certain types of baking pans are necessary.

   o **Bread pans** for loaves are a good choice. To get the optimum loaf of bread, bread made using 3 cups of flour should be in an 8½-by-4½-inch pan, while a loaf made with 4 cups of flour should be baked in a 9-by-5-inch pan.

   o A **large rimmed sheet pan** is added to the oven, along with the bread, onto which ice is added to produce steam.

   o A **baking sheet** or **baking stone** is perfect for baguettes and other shaped breads.

   o **9-by-13-inch** baking dish

o **Bread lame (tool with a handle to hold razor blades)** or **very sharp knife:** Use either utensil to slash the bread dough tops.

o **6-quart Dutch oven:** This size is the perfect pan to use for baking round loaves of sourdough bread. The sourdough bread loaf is placed in the pan where it is lightly sprayed with water and then covered. Halfway through the baking time, remove the lid to allow a hearty top crust to develop.

o **Food scale:** A digital (more precise than other types) food scale isn't absolutely necessary, but using one increases the chance of sourdough success. Besides weighing ingredients for accurate measure, a scale can be very useful when dividing dough or starter into equal parts.

o **Food thermometer:** A digital food thermometer is extremely important to measure water and dough temperatures.

o **Measuring cups and spoons (dry and liquid):** You will still need them even with a scale.

o **Mixing bowls:** Stainless steel mixing bowls are perfect as long as they are not used to store sourdough starter (see page 6).

o **Oven:** It doesn't have to be a full-size oven, but full-size ovens tend to be better sealed than a countertop toaster/convection oven combination.

o **Oven thermometer:** An oven thermometer is necessary when using the oven to proof bread dough. Checking the oven's calibration every once in a while isn't a bad idea either.

In addition to the equipment already listed, check to be sure you have at least the following essential equipment on hand. You can add more as your baking enthusiasm grows.

Essential Equipment

o 4-quart and 1-quart glass or plastic containers to store starter

o Dough scraper

o Kitchen towels

o Knives: bread or serrated

o Rubber spatula

o Spray bottle

o Wire rack

Useful but Not Essential Equipment

o Baking stone

o Baguette pan

o Banneton (proofing basket)

o Breadboard

o Bread machine

o Danish dough whisk

o Electric handheld mixer

o Electric knife

o Food processor

o Pizza peel

o Pullman bread pan (includes a cover)

o Stand mixer

Wish List

o Double oven

o Grain mill (for making your own flour)

o Proofing box

How to Adjust the Sour in Sourdough

Many people avoid sourdough bread because they don't enjoy food with a sour flavor. Sourdough bread doesn't have to be overly sour. There are several ways to adjust the sourness of the bread.

Prefer a more sour bread? Do the opposite of the following instructions.

1. **Choose your flour wisely.** Rye flour already has a sour flavor, which intensifies through the fermentation process. Don't use rye flour in the starter process. Still want to make a rye bread? Only add it to the bread dough in equal or lesser proportion to white bread flour.

2. **Adjust the feeding schedule.** A sourdough starter, when fed more frequently, produces less sourness in the starter.

3. **Try adding one of these ingredients.** Recipes for bread doughs that use baker's yeast and/or baking soda lessen the sour flavor. The baker's yeast causes the bread to rise faster, alleviating the need for additional risings, which naturally produce more bacteria and enzymes, which cause the sour flavor. Baking soda naturally neutralizes acid. The acid formed in sourdough is what makes the bread sour.

Getting Ready for Your First Bake

The day has finally arrived. After almost a week of feeding your sourdough starter, it is ready to use. Where do you go from here? What else do you need to know before making that first epic loaf? You will find several items here to consider.

Be Sure Your Starter Is Well-Fed and Ready to Use

After feeding your sourdough starter for days, you've finally achieved success. You have a jar with what looks like a light brown sponge that has doubled in size and smells delightfully sour. Now is the time to start the bread baking process. All recipes require that when baking with a sourdough starter, it needs to be active and well fed. The final feeding is done between 6 and 12 hours before mixing it with the other bread dough ingredients. If your starter peaked a few days before and you didn't have time to start the bread making process, you may have decided to refrigerate it, feeding it only weekly. If so, leave it on the counter for 1 hour or so before giving it its final feeding.

Measure in Weight

Flour measured with a measuring cup is never an exact measurement. Some people use the measuring cup as a scoop, packing the flour into it. That ensures that too much flour is added to the baked good. Others may lightly spoon flour into the cup and level off the top as directed—but how packed is the flour in the spoon? Is there enough in the cup?

For the beginning baker, there is a much better chance of sourdough success when the flour is weighed. With most scales you can use the tare weight, meaning the receptacle that holds the flour isn't counted in the weight. My scale has two options for accomplishing this: You put the receptacle on the scale and turn it on. It will begin with zero. The amount of flour needed for the recipe is then added. If the scale is already on, place the receptacle on it and then hit the "Tare" button. This will zero out the weight on the scale. If you use a piece of parchment paper to hold your flour, you probably will get a zero weight either way.

Water Temperature Is Key

It is important to use pure filtered or bottled water, but the temperature of the water is important, too. The water added in the dough-making process should be room temperature (75°F). If the water is too cold, the dough will take forever to rise. If the water is too warm, you won't get an even rise. It is important to invest in a digital thermometer not only for taking the temperature of the water, but also for taking the temperature of the dough, which should maintain a temperature of 75°F.

Air Temperature Is Critical

It's a beautiful day and the windows are open, letting the cool breezes blow throughout the house. This is wonderful for you, but not your rising bread dough. Cool breezes don't allow for an even dough rise. An overly warm kitchen is also bad for proofing and resting. Finding a place to keep your dough at 75°F is very important. I like to use a cold oven and turn on the light. Place an oven thermometer inside the oven to make sure it doesn't get too warm. If it does, turn off the light.

Time as an Ingredient

As important as any ingredient is time, beginning with creation of the starter and ending with removal of that prized loaf from the oven. After I have an established sourdough starter, I find the easiest way to schedule baking sourdough is on a day I'm off or can get off work early. If applicable, schedule time (in reverse order) for continued baking for the crust, baking for the steaming, final rising, kneading, rising, mixing, final starter feed, and starter making. Again, making sourdough bread is ideal for the beginning baker because it isn't difficult—it's just time consuming.

How Environment Affects Sourdough Starter Enzymes and Baking

A sourdough starter develops when the wild yeast from whole-grain flour combines with lactic acid, a good bacterium, found in the air. If the ingredients and the air are too cool, it takes longer for the sourdough starter to grow. If the ingredients and the environment are too warm, the starter will grow faster, but you'll need to discard more of it before each feeding. If the temperature gets as high as 180°F, your starter will die. The ideal temperatures for maintaining a sourdough starter are between 75°F and 80°F.

Your First Sourdough Dough

Once you've mastered your schedule, it won't be long before you're eating a warm, crusty piece of homemade sourdough bread. The following steps demonstrate how simple the process is.

1. **Mix:** Combine the sourdough with the other bread dough ingredients with your hands, a spoon, or an electric mixer. The key is not to overmix the ingredients, but you must incorporate all the flour into the dough.

2. **Knead:** Different recipes have different kneading processes.

   o If you're dealing with a wet dough, such as a 100 percent hydration loaf, use your bread scraper to knead right in the bowl, using the scoop-and-stretch method: With the scraper, scoop under the dough and stretch it out the other side.

   o Another method for wet dough is the folding method, which is also used to form a dough ball. This is accomplished by using well-floured hands to shape the dough into a slightly flattened oval on a floured breadboard or work surface.

From the top of the oval, pull the dough down three-fourths of the way to the bottom of the oval. Turn the dough and repeat. Keep repeating until you've kneaded the bread for the number of times indicated in the recipe.

o   If you're making a regular bread dough, you can knead it by hand or in the bowl of a stand mixer fitted with the dough hook, starting on the lowest speed so as not to overmix the dough. You can also use a bread machine for the mixing and kneading. You have the option of removing the dough from the machine and letting it shape and rise in a traditional baking pan.

3. **First rise:** Sometimes the first rise happens just after the dough ingredients are mixed. It's usually a combination of dough rest and rise. This is done according to the time required in the recipe.

4. **Shape:** The dough is shaped according to the type of bread and bread pan you are using. The folding method mentioned previously (see page 24) is typically how dough is shaped. Folding allows the bread to rise better.

5. **Proof:** Proofing is when the dough is allowed to rise in a warm, draft-free environment. I like to use the oven with only the light as a heat source.

6. **Score:** Just before baking, the top of your sourdough bread loaf must be scored. Using a bread lame or very sharp knife, score (cut into) the dough. By doing this, you're choosing where the bread will rise. Out of the top of the loaf is preferred.

7. **Bake:** Breads baked in a Dutch oven have two baking times. The first allows the loaf to be steamed with the pot lid on; during the second, the lid is removed to allow the crust to brown.

8. **Cool and serve:** Let your bread cool in the pan on a wire rack. Resist cutting into your lovely loaf until it cools. If you just can't take it, here's a tip: Use an electric knife to cut the warm bread—you'll end up with good slices instead of gummy ones.

9. **Store:** Sourdough bread doesn't mold as fast as other breads due to the fermentation in the starter. Purists keep their leftover sourdough bread in an old-fashioned bread box. An empty microwave makes a good substitute. If you decide to keep your bread tightly wrapped in plastic, keep in mind the crust will soften. Sourdough bread can be frozen for up to three months without losing any of its lovely flavor. To avoid freezer burn, wrap the loaf in plastic and then put it in a resealable freezer bag. Unwrap the bread entirely and place it in an empty microwave to defrost it completely.

Method: Ambient versus Retarded Proofing

All sourdough bread dough must be proofed—allowed to rise—before baking. Proofing is accomplished by using either an ambient (warm) method or a retarded (cool) method. Many recipes use both methods. The ambient method is typically the first proofing required, and the retarded method is used in the final proofing.

Ambient

Ambient proofing is done in warm temperatures, between 75°F and 80°F. If your kitchen is particularly warm, the dough could be proofed on the kitchen counter. Most home kitchens aren't typically that warm unless a lot of baking is being done. If your kitchen is cooler, a simple method of getting the right temperature is to turn the oven light on. Place your dough in a bowl, cover it with a clean kitchen towel, and place it in the oven. Place an oven thermometer on the rack, where you can see it through the glass door. Verify the temperature isn't getting too high. If it is, turn off the light.

Retarded

Retarded proofing, generally the final proofing, is accomplished by refrigerating the already-shaped dough in an airtight container at 40°F overnight. The next day, remove the dough from the refrigerator and place it in or on its baking receptacle. Allow it to sit on the counter for an hour or so to warm up a little before baking.

How to Tell If Your Dough Is Ready to Bake

The best way to test if it's time to bake your sourdough loaf is after the second rising. As directed, shape your dough loaf for the type of bread you are baking. Place it in the pan, if applicable. Cover it with a floured kitchen towel and put it in a warm place to rise for the allotted time.

Place the risen dough on the counter. Give it a minute and lightly push the dough on the side or top with your thumb. The indentation should fill up halfway; if not, let it rise a little longer (30 minutes to 1 hour). If either fills all the way, allow for a second rise.

Sourdough Bread Number 1

All sourdough breads are time consuming, but this simple recipe can be baked within 12 hours, if your sourdough starter is already established. ***Makes 1 round boule***

FOR ACTIVATING THE STARTER

4¾ ounces (½ cup) sourdough starter

4 ounces (½ cup) lukewarm (90°F to 100°F) pure filtered or bottled water

4 ounces (scant 1 cup) unbleached bread flour

FOR THE BREAD DOUGH

12¾ ounces (3 cups) unbleached bread flour, plus more for dusting

10 ounces (1¼ cups) lukewarm (90°F to 100°F) pure filtered or bottled water

7 ounces (¾ cup) active sourdough starter

1 teaspoon salt

Olive oil or nonstick cooking spray, for preparing the bowl

PRE-PREP TIME: STARTER CREATION 5 DAYS, PLUS 6 TO 12 HOURS TO ACTIVATE THE STARTER

SOURDOUGH METHOD: AMBIENT

PREP TIME: 5 HOURS 45 MINUTES

BAKING TIME: 24 TO 27 MINUTES

TOTAL TIME: 6 HOURS 12 MINUTES

Tools needed

6-quart Dutch oven, bread lame or very sharp knife, mixing bowls, spray bottle

To activate the starter

At least 6 to 12 hours before making the dough, in a medium bowl, combine the starter, lukewarm water, and flour, completely incorporating the ingredients into the starter. Loosely cover and let sit on the counter until ready to use.

To make the bread dough

1. In a large bowl, stir together the flour, water, and active starter. Cover the bowl with a clean kitchen towel and let rest for 20 minutes.

2. Sprinkle the salt over the top of the dough and, in the bowl, knead it in. Continue to knead for at least 8 to 10 minutes more.

3. Lightly coat a large bowl with olive oil and transfer the dough to it, turning to coat all sides. Cover the bowl with a clean kitchen towel and put it in a warm place to rise for 90 minutes. (Don't have a warm place? Place your bowl in the oven with the light on.)

➤

4. Flour a breadboard or clean work surface and turn the dough out on to it. Press the dough into an oval shape. Fold the dough over a couple of times by grabbing the right side of the dough and pulling it to the left side. Grab the top part and pull it to the bottom. Re-cover and let rise for another 90 minutes.

5. One last time, slightly push the dough into an oval shape. Grab the top part of the oval and pull it down three-fourths of the way to the bottom of the oval. Give the dough a quarter turn. Pull the top of the oval three-fourths of the way to the bottom. Make another quarter turn and repeat as often as it takes to form a ball. Place the dough, seam-side up, in the bowl. Re-cover and let rise for 2 hours more in a warm place.

6. Remove the dough bowl from the oven, if that's where it's been rising.

7. Place your Dutch oven, with its lid on, in the center of the oven. Preheat the oven to 450°F.

8. On a breadboard or counter, place a square of parchment paper and lightly flour it. Place the bread dough into the center of the parchment. Shape the dough in an oval once again. Fold the top down almost all the way to the bottom. Turn the dough a quarter turn. Fold down once again, almost to the bottom. Turn again. Repeat until all sides are done. If the dough is too sticky, add a bit of flour as you go. Sprinkle the top with a bit of flour and smooth it out. Cover the dough with a clean kitchen towel and let rest for 15 minutes.

9. Test the dough by sticking your thumb into the side of the bread dough. If the indention springs back it's ready. If it's not ready, let it rest a bit longer.

10. Using a bread lame or very sharp knife, slash the top of the bread.

11. Carefully, using oven gloves, slide out the shelf with the Dutch oven on it. Remove the lid and place it on the stovetop. Using the corners of the parchment, transfer the bread dough and parchment into the hot pot. Spray the bread with water a couple of times and place the lid on the Dutch oven. Return it to the oven and bake for 12 minutes.

12. Carefully remove the lid from the pot and continue baking for 12 to 15 minutes more, or until the crust is a golden brown. Remove the pot from the oven. Carefully remove the lid and transfer the bread on the parchment to a wire rack to cool. Resist cutting into the bread until it's safe to touch without being burned.

Variations: Nearly any other bread flour type may be used with this recipe.

Common Problems and FAQs

Q: Why did my loaf come out so dense?
A: The bread starter is what creates the holes in the bread. If the bread dough was overmixed, the starter may have been overmixed as well.

Q: Why didn't my bread rise enough?
A: There are several reasons your bread didn't rise properly. Your sourdough starter wasn't active when using it in your dough. Active sourdough helps the bread rise. Another reason is the ingredients must be measured properly. Too much water or flour can affect the bread. When measuring ingredients, use a digital scale to weigh them for accuracy. Lastly, your oven may not be calibrated properly. Test your oven temperature with an oven thermometer before beginning the baking process.

Q: Why did my loaf rise horizontally instead of vertically?
A: You may not have scored your loaf before baking. You get to choose how the bread rises when you score the top of the bread.

100% Hydration Simple Sourdough Boule

This sourdough loaf recipe produces a wetter dough than most other recipes. To compensate for the wet dough, a different kneading method is used, plus the dough is not kneaded as often as in other recipes. ***Makes 1 round boule***

FOR ACTIVATING THE STARTER

4¾ ounces (½ cup) sourdough starter

4 ounces (½ cup) lukewarm (90°F to 100°F) pure filtered or bottled water

4 ounces (scant 1 cup) unbleached bread flour

FOR THE BREAD DOUGH

12¾ ounces (3 cups) unbleached bread flour, plus more for dusting

1¼ teaspoons fine sea salt

2.4 ounces (¼ cup) active sourdough starter

10½ ounces (1⅓ cups) cool (60°F to 70°F) pure filtered or bottled water

PRE-PREP TIME: STARTER CREATION 5 DAYS, PLUS 6 TO 12 HOURS TO ACTIVATE THE STARTER

SOURDOUGH METHOD: AMBIENT

PREP TIME: 15 HOURS 40 MINUTES

BAKING TIME: 50 MINUTES

TOTAL TIME: 16 HOURS 30 MINUTES

Tools needed

6-quart Dutch oven, bread lame or very sharp knife, mixing bowls, banneton basket or colander, spray bottle

To activate the starter

At least 6 to 12 hours before making the dough, in a medium bowl, combine the starter, lukewarm water, and flour, completely incorporating the ingredients into the starter. Loosely cover and let sit on the counter until ready to use.

To make the bread dough

1. In a large bowl, stir together the flour and salt. Add the active starter and cool water and mix completely until combined. Cover the bowl with a clean kitchen towel and let rise on the counter for at least 12 hours. If the dough has not doubled in size, let it rest a bit longer.

2. Since this dough is so wet, it's better to knead the dough right in the bowl. Tilt the bowl toward you. Use your dough scraper to move all the dough toward the front of the bowl. Keeping the bowl tilted, scrape the dough scraper from under the dough in the back of the bowl toward the front, lifting the dough as you get it all the way to the front of the bowl. Do this continuously for about 10 minutes.

3. Lightly flour a breadboard or clean work surface, turn the dough out on to it, and turn the dough over a couple of times to coat it entirely with flour. With floured hands, take the top part of the dough and pull it three-fourths of the way toward you. Turn the dough and do this again, and at least four more times, to form a ball.

4. Line a colander with a clean kitchen towel or a banneton basket with the cloth that comes with it. Evenly spray the cloth with water. Cover the wet cloth generously with flour. Make sure you have a good layer of flour so the dough won't stick. Roll the dough one more time in the flour and place it in the basket, seam-side up. Loosely cover with a clean kitchen towel and let rise for 2 to 3 hours.

5. Preheat the oven to 475°F. Place your Dutch oven, with its lid on, in the oven to preheat for 30 minutes.

6. While the oven heats, it's time to remove the dough from the basket or colander. Hold a square piece of parchment paper over the top of the basket. Place a small cutting board or a large plate, inverted, on top of the parchment. Carefully flip the risen dough. Remove the basket. Your dough should have the design from the colander or basket in it. Using a bread lame or very sharp knife, cut an X into the top of the bread dough.

➤

7. Using oven gloves, carefully pull out the rack with the Dutch oven on it. Remove the lid and place it on the stovetop. Using the corners of the parchment, transfer the bread dough and parchment into the hot pot. Spray the bread with water a couple of times and re-cover the pot. Place it into the oven and bake for 30 minutes.

8. Remove the lid and bake the bread for 15 to 20 minutes more until the crust is golden brown.

9. Transfer the bread to a wire rack and let cool completely before slicing.

Common Problems and FAQs

Q: Why was my dough so sticky and slack?
A: Because there was more water in the dough than flour. You don't want to add too much flour to correct the problem, as you'll end up with a dry loaf of bread.

Q: What is the correct flour to water ratio?
A: There isn't a correct flour to water ratio. Different recipes call for different ratios. As an example, a ciabatta (page 102) is a flat bread with big holes in it. It is a very wet dough, but that is the correct result from the recipe.

Q: Why did my high hydration loaf taste so different?
A: The holes in the bread are bigger and so you taste "less" bread in each bite.

PART TWO
The Recipes

You've made and maintained your own personal sourdough starter for a while now. You may have baked a loaf or two, and you're ready for a little adventure. Here are the recipes to explore the full potential of your sourdough starter—everything from traditional artisan and rustic bread loaves to dinner rolls and sandwich buns. Go down the healthy whole food road by baking sourdough loaves with seeds and exotic flours. You'll discover that just about anything made with flour can be made tastier with your very own personal sourdough starter. Let your sourdough starter adventures begin!

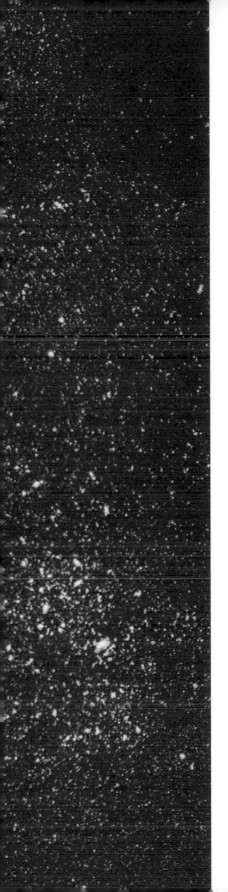

Chapter Three
RUSTIC AND ARTISAN LOAVES

Do you envision a round loaf of crusty bread—with soft insides and big holes—when thinking about rustic and artisan breads? They are similar in that they are both made with few, but fresh, ingredients. Typically, bread described as "rustic" is hand formed, not baked in a pan. Artisan bread sounds like something made by a food artist. If you are dreaming of a rustic or artisanal bread dripping with butter or extra-virgin olive oil, the recipes in this chapter are for you.

Classic Whole-Wheat Artisan Bread

Everyone needs at least one recipe for a comforting whole-wheat sourdough bread, and this is it. It makes loaves that are a bit softer than most artisan breads and that have a honey taste. I recommend that you use a good-quality local honey. ***Makes 2 loaves***

FOR ACTIVATING THE STARTER

19 ounces (2 cups) sourdough starter

8 ounces (1 cup) lukewarm (90°F to 100°F) pure filtered or bottled water

8 ounces (2 cups) whole-wheat flour

FOR THE BREAD DOUGH

19 ounces (2 cups) active sourdough starter

26 ounces (5½ cups) whole-grain whole-wheat flour

8 ounces (1 cup) milk (whole or 2 percent)

4 ounces (½ cup) room temperature (75°F) pure filtered or bottled water

4 ounces (1 stick) good quality butter, melted and cooled

3 ounces (¼ cup) honey, preferably local

2½ teaspoons fine sea salt

Olive oil or nonstick cooking spray, for preparing the bowls, bread pans, and spraying the loaves

PRE-PREP TIME: 6 TO 12 HOURS TO ACTIVATE THE STARTER

SUGGESTED STARTER: WHOLE WHEAT

SOURDOUGH METHOD: AMBIENT

PREP TIME: 9 HOURS 40 MINUTES

BAKING TIME: 30 TO 35 MINUTES

TOTAL TIME: 10 HOURS 15 MINUTES

Tools needed

two 8½-by-4½-inch bread pans, bread lame or very sharp knife

To activate the starter

At least 6 to 12 hours before making the dough, in a medium bowl, combine the starter, lukewarm water, and flour, completely incorporating the ingredients into the starter. Loosely cover and let sit on the counter until ready to use.

To make the bread dough

1. In a large bowl, stir together the active starter, whole-grain flour, milk, room temperature water, butter, and honey. Let the dough rest for 20 minutes.

2. Add the salt and, in the bowl, knead it in, kneading for at least 5 minutes. If the dough is too sticky, knead it a bit longer.

3. Generously coat a large bowl with olive oil and transfer the dough to it, turning to coat all sides. Cover the bowl with a clean kitchen towel and place it in a warm, draft-free place. Let the dough rise for at least 3 hours. The dough should double in size.

4. Coat two 8½-by-4½-inch bread pans with cooking spray and set aside.

5. Lightly flour a breadboard or clean work surface and turn the dough out on to it. Divide the dough in half. Shape the dough pieces about the same size as the bread pans you are using. Now, pull the ends, picking up the dough and slapping it onto the surface as you lengthen the dough until it's twice the size of the bread pan. Fold one end of the dough over one-third of the way across the loaf. Fold the other end over one-third of the way. At the end near you, press down to seal the fold. Starting at the top of the dough, roll it in toward you, about four times until the dough is about the size of the bread pan. Lightly roll the dough back and forth to even out the loaf. Place the dough in one of the prepared bread pans. Repeat the dough-shaping steps with the remaining piece of dough. Spray each loaf with olive oil and cover with plastic wrap. Let rise for 2 to 3 hours.

6. Preheat the oven to 400°F.

7. Using a bread lame or very sharp knife, slash the top of each loaf. Bake for 30 to 35 minutes, or until the bread is browned on top, sounds hollow when tapped with your finger, and reaches an internal temperature of around 205°F on a digital food thermometer.

8. Cool the bread in the pans for 5 to 10 minutes. Remove from the pans and transfer to a wire rack to cool completely.

Tip: What makes a homemade bread, especially this Classic Whole-Wheat Artisan Bread, special? Serving it with honey butter. In a small bowl, using a handheld electric mixer, whip 4 ounces (1 stick) of room-temperature butter and 3 ounces (¼ cup) of locally sourced honey. Store any leftover honey butter in the refrigerator or on the counter, if your kitchen isn't too warm.

Sourdough Rustic Rosemary Bread

Living in the southern part of the United States, I'm lucky to be able to grow rosemary all year. If you don't live in a warm climate year-round, know that rosemary will survive a few days of below-freezing temperatures. ***Makes 2 loaves***

FOR ACTIVATING THE STARTER

4¾ ounces (½ cup) sourdough starter

4 ounces (½ cup) lukewarm (90°F to 100°F) pure filtered or bottled water

4 ounces (1 cup) whole-wheat flour

FOR THE BREAD DOUGH

21¼ ounces (5 cups) unbleached bread flour, unbleached all-purpose flour, or rye flour

9½ ounces (1 cup) active sourdough starter

12 ounces (1½ cups) lukewarm (90°F to 100°F) water

2½ teaspoons fine sea salt

2 teaspoons instant dry yeast

0.2 ounces (¼ cup) chopped fresh rosemary, plus more for garnishing (optional)

Olive oil or nonstick cooking spray, for preparing the bowl

Pink Himalayan salt or another coarse salt, for garnishing (optional)

PRE-PREP TIME: 6 TO 12 HOURS TO ACTIVATE THE STARTER

SUGGESTED STARTER: WHOLE WHEAT

SOURDOUGH METHOD: AMBIENT

PREP TIME: 1 HOUR 46 MINUTES

BAKING TIME: 30 MINUTES

TOTAL TIME: 2 HOURS 16 MINUTES

Tools needed

baking stone or heavy baking sheet, bread lame or very sharp knife, spray bottle

To activate the starter

At least 6 to 12 hours before making the dough, in a medium bowl, combine the starter, lukewarm water, and flour, completely incorporating the ingredients into the starter. Loosely cover and let sit on the counter until ready to use.

To make the bread dough

1. In a large bowl, stir together the flour, active starter, lukewarm water, sea salt, yeast, and rosemary until combined. Knead the dough, in the bowl, for 12 to 16 minutes until smooth on the surface, but still a bit sticky. Form the dough into a ball.

2. Coat a clean large bowl with olive oil and transfer the bread dough to it, turning to coat all sides. Loosely cover the top of the bowl with plastic wrap and place the bowl in the oven with only the light turned on. Do not turn on the oven. Let the dough rise for at least 90 minutes. It should double in size.

3. Remove the bowl from the oven.

4. Place a baking stone or heavy baking sheet into the oven. Preheat the oven to 425°F.

5. Punch the dough down and divide it in half, forming each half into a rectangle. Working with one rectangle, grab the longest side and fold it halfway toward you. Press the edge slightly and fold in half one more time, toward you. Be sure to tuck the edges underneath the roll. Repeat with the other rectangle. Using a bread lame or very sharp knife, cut angled slashes into each log.

6. Spray the loaves with warm (100°F to 125°F) water. Sprinkle each loaf with Himalayan salt and fresh rosemary, if you like.

7. Flour parchment paper and put the loaves on it. Carefully pick up the parchment paper with the bread on it and place it on the baking stone. Generously spray both sides of the oven with water right before closing the oven door.

8. Bake for 25 to 30 minutes, or until the crusts are golden brown. Carefully transfer to a wire rack to cool completely before slicing. If you must slice the bread before it's completely cool, use an electric bread knife so as not to crush the bread as you're holding it.

Tip: To verify that your starter is active, do the float test. Place a spoonful of starter into a glass of water. If it floats, it's ready. If it doesn't float, feed your starter with equal amounts of flour and water 6 to 12 hours before using it in this recipe.

San Francisco Treat

Some people say you can't make real San Francisco sourdough bread unless you live in San Francisco. You must be a part of the environment and use the wild yeast located there. Well, maybe that is true, but I believe this bread comes pretty close. I remember having a San Francisco sourdough bread boule with the center hollowed out. There was steam coming out of the top. Inside was some of the best clam chowder I've ever eaten. Between the bread and the soup, I think at the time life couldn't get much better. ***Makes 2 round boules***

FOR ACTIVATING THE STARTER

4¾ ounces (½ cup) sourdough starter

4 ounces (½ cup) lukewarm (90°F to 100°F) pure filtered or bottled water

4 ounces (1 cup) whole-wheat flour

FOR THE BREAD DOUGH

1 pound (scant 4 cups) unbleached bread flour

9½ ounces (1 cup) active sourdough starter

8 ounces (1 cup) room temperature (75°F) pure filtered or bottled water

1 ounce (2 tablespoons) good quality olive oil

2¼ teaspoons fine sea salt

Semolina or cornmeal, for dusting

PRE-PREP TIME: 6 TO 12 HOURS TO ACTIVATE THE STARTER

SUGGESTED STARTER: WHOLE WHEAT

SOURDOUGH METHOD: AMBIENT

PREP TIME: 4 HOURS 33 MINUTES

BAKING TIME: 35 MINUTES

TOTAL TIME: 5 HOURS 8 MINUTES

Tools needed

stand mixer, two 6-quart Dutch ovens, bread lame or very sharp knife, spray bottle

To activate the starter

At least 6 to 12 hours before making the dough, in a medium bowl, combine the starter, lukewarm water, and flour, completely incorporating the ingredients into the starter. Loosely cover and let sit on the counter until ready to use.

To make the bread dough

1. In the bowl of a stand mixer fitted with a dough hook, or in a large bowl, combine the flour, active starter, room temperature water, and olive oil. Mix the ingredients on low speed for about 1 minute, or by hand until combined. Once combined, let the dough rest in the bowl for at least 30 minutes.

2. Add the salt and mix on low speed for 1 minute, or by hand for 2 minutes. Increase the speed to medium and mix for 2 minutes more, or 4 minutes by hand. Stop the machine. Remove any loose dough from the hook and return it to the bowl. If necessary, scrape the inside of the bowl to make sure the dough is in one piece.

3. Cover the bowl with a clean kitchen towel and let rise for 2 hours. The dough should double in size. If it has not risen, wait another 15 minutes or so until it does.

4. Once the dough has doubled in size, divide it into two equal pieces. Form each into a ball by continually tucking the edges of the dough underneath until the top is tight and it's shaped like a ball.

5. Line two Dutch ovens with parchment paper and generously sprinkle the parchment with semolina or cornmeal (this keeps the bread from sticking, and the flavor from the semolina or the cornmeal won't affect the taste of the bread), and place one dough ball in each pot, seam-side down. Re-cover the dough and let rise for 1 to 2 hours more.

6. Preheat the oven to 400°F.

7. Using a bread lame or a very sharp knife, cut an X into the top of each loaf. Don't be afraid to cut down into the loaf. Spray the bread with water a couple of times and place the lids on the pots. Bake for 20 minutes.

8. Remove the lids and bake for 10 to 15 minutes more.

9. Remove from the oven and let the bread cool for 5 minutes in the pots. Lifting the loaves using the corners of the parchment, carefully transfer the bread to wire racks to cool completely before slicing.

Tip: For baking at a later date, you can freeze one of your boules. Place your shaped dough in the freezer on a parchment paper–lined baking sheet. Let it freeze overnight. Remove the bread dough from the freezer. Wrap it in plastic wrap and put it in a sturdy freezer bag. Place it back in the freezer, where it will keep for three months without losing any flavor.

The day before baking, let the dough defrost first in the refrigerator. Place the dough in a heavily floured proofing basket or colander, cover with a floured kitchen towel, and let rise 2 hours before baking according to the recipe instructions.

Perfect Italian Sourdough

Semolina is very similar to cornmeal in looks and texture. While cornmeal is made from corn, semolina is made from wheat. Even though it's a wheat, the semolina gives this bread a nutty texture. Sprinkling it over the bread top amplifies that texture. ***Makes 1 loaf***

FOR ACTIVATING THE STARTER

4¾ ounces (½ cup) sourdough starter

4 ounces (½ cup) lukewarm (90°F to 100°F) pure filtered or bottled water

4 ounces (1 cup) whole-wheat flour

FOR THE BREAD DOUGH

9½ ounces (1 cup) active sourdough starter

8 ounces (1 cup) warm (100°F to 125°F) pure filtered or bottled water

6 ounces (1½ cups) fine semolina flour, plus more for dusting the pan and the loaf (optional)

4 ounces (scant 1 cup) unbleached bread flour, plus more for dusting

2 teaspoons fine sea salt

Olive oil, for preparing the bowl

Nonstick cooking spray, for preparing the bread pan and plastic bag

1 egg, lightly beaten (optional)

PRE-PREP TIME: 6 TO 12 HOURS TO ACTIVATE THE STARTER

SUGGESTED STARTER: WHOLE WHEAT

SOURDOUGH METHOD: RETARDED

PREP TIME: 6 HOURS 6 MINUTES, PLUS OVERNIGHT IN THE REFRIGERATOR

BAKING TIME: 35 MINUTES

TOTAL TIME: 6 HOURS 41 MINUTES, PLUS OVERNIGHT IN THE REFRIGERATOR

Tools needed

stand mixer, 9-by-5-inch bread pan, bread lame or very sharp knife

To activate the starter

At least 6 to 12 hours prior to making the dough, in a medium bowl, combine the starter, lukewarm water, and flour, completely incorporating the ingredients into the starter. Loosely cover and let sit on the counter until ready to use.

To make the bread dough

1. In the bowl of a stand mixer fitted with the dough hook, or a large bowl and using a handheld electric mixer, combine the active starter, warm water, semolina flour, bread flour, and salt. Mix on low speed for at least 3 minutes until the ingredients are completely combined. If mixing by hand, mix for 6 minutes.

2. Coat a large bowl with olive oil and transfer the dough to it, turning to coat all sides. Cover the bowl with a clean kitchen towel and let rise for 5 to 6 hours, or until it doubles in size.

3. Coat a baking pan with cooking spray and sprinkle the bottom with semolina. Coat a large resealable plastic bag with cooking spray. Set both aside.

4. Lightly flour a breadboard or clean work surface and turn the dough out on to it. With your hands, stretch out the dough. Fold it in half and stretch it again. Shape the dough into a rectangle, making sure the shortest end is not wider than the length of a 9-by-5-inch pan. From the short end roll the dough so it will fit nicely in the bread pan. Brush the top with the beaten egg (if using) and sprinkle the top with about 2 tablespoons of semolina flour, if desired.

5. Place the bread pan in the prepared plastic bag and refrigerate overnight.

6. The next morning, remove the bread pan from the refrigerator. Let sit on the counter for 1 hour or so. Using a bread lame or very sharp knife, slash the top of the loaf.

7. Preheat the oven to 400°F.

8. Bake the bread for 35 minutes, or until it reaches an internal temperature of 200°F on a digital food thermometer.

9. Let the bread cool in the pan for 10 minutes. Remove the bread and transfer to a wire rack to cool completely before slicing.

Tip: Instead of serving this bread with butter, try olive oil. Fill a small bowl with a good quality olive oil. Add equal amounts of grated Parmesan cheese and Italian seasoning. Serve a salad with this bread and no one will want anything else for dinner.

Roasted Garlic Sourdough Bread

The roasted garlic imparts brilliant flavor to this bread. You can buy roasted garlic in a jar, but why? It is so easy to roast it yourself. The instructions are found at the end of this recipe. ***Makes 1 loaf***

FOR ACTIVATING THE STARTER

4¾ ounces (½ cup) sourdough starter

4 ounces (½ cup) lukewarm (90°F to 100°F) pure filtered or bottled water

4 ounces (1 cup) whole-wheat flour

FOR THE BREAD DOUGH

2.4 ounces (¼ cup) active sourdough starter

12 ounces (1½ cups) warm (100°F to 125°F) pure filtered or bottled water

1 pound (scant 4 cups) unbleached bread flour, plus more for dusting

2 ounces (½ cup) whole-wheat flour

1½ teaspoons fine sea salt

1 head garlic, roasted (see tip)

PRE-PREP TIME: 6 TO 12 HOURS TO ACTIVATE THE STARTER, PLUS 30 MINUTES FOR ROASTING THE GARLIC

SUGGESTED STARTER: WHOLE WHEAT

SOURDOUGH METHOD: AMBIENT

PREP TIME: 9 HOURS

BAKING TIME: 40 MINUTES

TOTAL TIME: 9 HOURS 40 MINUTES

Tools needed

6-quart Dutch oven, bread lame or very sharp knife, spray bottle

To activate the starter

At least 6 to 12 hours prior to making the dough, in a medium bowl, combine the starter, lukewarm water, and flour, completely incorporating the ingredients into the starter. Loosely cover and let sit on the counter until ready to use.

To make the bread dough

1. In a large bowl, stir together the active starter, warm water, bread flour, and whole-wheat flour, mixing until combined. Cover the bowl with a clean kitchen towel and let rest for 30 minutes.

2. Add the salt and, in the bowl, knead it in by folding the dough over and pushing on it. Continue kneading until the dough forms a smooth ball and begins to tighten. Spread the dough out a bit, add the roasted garlic cloves, and knead them in, trying to evenly distribute them without crushing.

3. Cover the dough with a clean damp kitchen towel and let rest at room temperature (about 75°F) until doubled in size, about 8 hours.

4. Lightly flour a breadboard or clean work surface and turn the dough out on to it. Using floured hands, shape the dough into a circle by continually tucking the edges under as you turn the ball.

5. Place the dough seam-side up into a well-floured banneton basket or into a small bowl lined with a well-floured kitchen towel. Cover the dough with another floured kitchen towel. Let rise for 30 minutes to 1 hour.

6. Preheat the oven to 450°F. Place a Dutch oven, with its lid on, in the oven.

7. Cut a square of parchment paper. Place it over the top of the dough. Carefully flip the bread dough onto the parchment paper. Sprinkle a little more flour over the top of the dough. Spread it evenly with your hands. Using a bread lame or very sharp knife, cut an X, or other design, into the top of the dough.

8. Reduce the oven temperature to 425°F.

9. Using oven gloves, pull out the rack with the Dutch oven on it. Remove the lid and place it on the stovetop. Using the corners of the parchment paper, transfer the dough and parchment into the hot pot. Spray the bread with water a couple of times and cover the pot. Bake for 30 minutes.

10. Using oven gloves, remove the lid and bake the bread for 10 minutes more.

➤

11. Remove the bread from the oven and let cool for a couple of minutes before transferring it to a wire rack to cool completely before slicing.

Option: Instead of proofing the bread dough for 8 hours (step 3), you can refrigerate it overnight. Just shape the dough into a ball and place it in the basket or bowl. Place the bread dough in an airtight bag and refrigerate overnight. Let the dough sit out for about 1 hour before you continue with the recipe.

Tip: Roasting Garlic

Preheat the oven to 400°F. Slice the top ½ inch off the pointed end of the garlic bulb. With your fingers, rub off as much of the paper from the outside of the bulb as possible. Place a square of aluminum foil on a baking sheet and set the garlic bulb in the middle. Drizzle the garlic with good quality olive oil. Pull up the sides of the foil and tightly wrap the garlic. Bake for 30 minutes. Remove from the oven and let cool. Remove the cloves from the bulb by gently pulling them off the core. Push each clove out of its paper home by pressing on the closed end. Set the roasted cloves aside until needed.

Greek Olive and Thribi Sourdough Bread

Get a taste of the Greek islands with this recipe. Thribi is the Greek version of oregano, and it's only grown there. If you're unable to purchase thribi, oregano will work. The Greek olives in this recipe are Kalamata olives. They are a black–deep purple olive with a powerful taste. Be sure to purchase pitted Kalamatas to save yourself time. The final Greek ingredient found in this recipe is kefalotiri, a very hard, nutty cheese typically shredded. If you have trouble finding it, Parmesan or Romano makes an acceptable substitute. ***Makes 1 round boule***

FOR ACTIVATING THE STARTER

2.4 ounces (¼ cup) sourdough starter

4 ounces (½ cup) lukewarm (90°F to 100°F) pure filtered or bottled water

4 ounces (1 cup) whole-wheat flour

FOR THE BREAD DOUGH

2.4 ounces (¼ cup) active sourdough starter

12 ounces (1½ cups) warm (100°F to 125°F) water

15 ounces (3½ cups) unbleached bread flour, plus more for dusting

2 ounces (½ cup) whole-grain whole-wheat flour

1 teaspoon fine sea salt

6½ ounces (1 cup) pitted Kalamata olives, quartered

1½ ounces (⅓ cup) grated kefalotiri cheese, or Parmesan or Romano cheese

2 teaspoons dried thribi, or oregano

PRE-PREP TIME: 6 TO 12 HOURS TO ACTIVATE THE STARTER

SUGGESTED STARTER: WHOLE WHEAT

SOURDOUGH METHOD: RETARDED

PREP TIME: 6 HOURS 30 MINUTES, PLUS OVERNIGHT IN THE REFRIGERATOR

BAKING TIME: 45 MINUTES

TOTAL TIME: 7 HOURS 15 MINUTES, PLUS OVERNIGHT IN THE REFRIGERATOR

Tools needed

6-quart Dutch oven, bread lame or very sharp knife, spray bottle

To activate the starter

At least 6 to 12 hours before making the dough, in a medium bowl, combine the starter, lukewarm water, and flour, completely incorporating the ingredients into the starter. Loosely cover and let sit on the counter until ready to use.

To make the bread dough

1. In a large bowl, stir together the active starter and warm water until the starter dissolves. Add the bread flour and whole-wheat flour to the bowl, mixing to combine completely, and let rest for 30 minutes.

2. Add the salt and mix it into the dough. Let the dough rest for 2 hours more.

➤

Rustic and Artisan Loaves   **49**

3. Gently knead the bread, in the bowl, a couple of times. Let rest for 2 hours more.

4. Knead it a couple of times again and let rest for 2 hours more.

5. After the 6 hours of intermittent kneading, knead in the olives, kefalotiri, and thribi until completely incorporated into the dough.

6. Place a parchment paper square on a flat surface and lightly flour it. Turn the bread dough out onto the prepared parchment. Work the dough by repeatedly pulling the corners of the dough toward the center to form a ball. Once the ball is achieved, turn it so the pulled edges are on the bottom. Using the parchment, transfer the bread dough to a clean bowl (with the parchment). The dough should bounce back when a finger is pushed into its side. Cover the bowl with a clean kitchen towel and refrigerate the dough overnight.

7. The next morning, preheat the oven to 450°F.

8. Remove the dough from the refrigerator. Sprinkle flour over the top of the bread and smooth it with your hand. Using a bread lame or very sharp knife, cut an X into the top of the dough.

9. Using the corners of the parchment, transfer the bread dough and parchment into a Dutch oven. Spray the bread with water a couple of times and place the lid on the pot. Bake for 10 minutes.

10. Reduce the oven temperature to 425°F and bake for 25 minutes more.

11. Remove the lid and bake for 10 minutes more. The bread is done when the crust is golden brown and the loaf reaches an internal temperature of 210°F on a digital food thermometer.

12. Transfer the pot to a wire rack and let the bread cool there for 10 to 15 minutes.

13. Remove the bread from the pan by lifting the parchment paper and place it on the wire rack to cool completely before slicing.

Tip: Serve this delicious savory bread as an appetizer at your next gathering. Line a baking sheet with aluminum foil. Cut the bread into ¾-inch slices. Continue to cut those pieces in halves or thirds depending on the overall size of each slice.

Place the bread on the prepared baking sheet. Place your oven rack in the highest position. Turn on the broiler. Place the baking sheet under the broiler but don't close the door all the way because you need to watch it. Once the bread browns around the edges, pull the pan out. Use a metal spatula to flip the slices. Place the baking sheet back in the oven, but do not completely close the door, and toast the other side. Place the toasted slices on a serving platter. Just before serving, lightly drizzle them with a good quality Greek olive oil. Sprinkle a little oregano over the slices before serving. If you prefer, spread butter on each slice, instead of the olive oil, before the second toasting. Be careful—the buttered bread will brown quickly.

Morning-Time Sourdough Bread

Although this loaf takes almost 24 hours to make, it's well worth it. It's loaded with lots of good-for-you things such as quinoa, oats, flax, and chia seeds. You'll find plenty of vegetable proteins here, too. ***Makes 1 Loaf***

FOR ACTIVATING THE STARTER

2.4 ounces (¼ cup) sourdough starter

4 ounces (½ cup) lukewarm (90°F to 100°F) pure filtered or bottled water

4 ounces (1 cup) whole-wheat flour or (1 heaping cup) rye flour

FOR THE BREAD DOUGH

Scant 1 ounce (¼ cup) quinoa, rinsed well

1½ ounces (¼ cup) steel cut oats

¾ ounce (¼ cup) old-fashioned rolled oats

1 tablespoon flaxseed

1 tablespoon chia seeds

¼ cup warm filtered water

9½ ounces (1 cup) active sourdough starter

4 ounces (½ cup) milk (whole or 2 percent)

2 ounces (¼ cup) room temperature (75°F) pure filtered or bottled water

2 tablespoons butter, melted and cooled

2 tablespoons honey, preferably locally sourced

10 ounces (2½ cups) whole-wheat or rye flour

Olive oil or nonstick cooking spray, for preparing the bowl and bread pan

1½ teaspoons fine sea salt

1 large egg (optional)

Sesame seeds, or pumpkin seeds, for garnishing (optional)

PRE-PREP TIME: 6 TO 12 HOURS TO ACTIVATE THE STARTER AND SOAK THE SEEDS

SUGGESTED STARTER: WHOLE WHEAT OR RYE

SOURDOUGH METHOD: RETARDED

PREP TIME: 3 HOURS 25 MINUTES, PLUS OVERNIGHT IN THE REFRIGERATOR

BAKING TIME: 35 MINUTES

TOTAL TIME: 4 HOURS, PLUS OVERNIGHT IN THE REFRIGERATOR

Tools needed

9-by-5-inch bread pan, bread lame or very sharp knife

To activate the starter

At least 6 to 12 hours before making the dough, in a medium bowl, combine the starter, lukewarm water, and flour, completely incorporating the ingredients into the starter. Loosely cover and let sit on the counter until ready to use.

To start the bread

At the same time you activate the starter, in a medium bowl combine the quinoa, oats, flaxseed, chia seeds, and water. Set aside and let soak for at least 8 hours.

To finish the bread

1. In a large bowl, combine the soaked seeds and oats, active starter, milk, room temperature water, butter, honey, and whole-wheat flour. Mix until completely combined. Cover the dough with a clean kitchen towel and let rest for 20 minutes.

2. Coat a large bowl with olive oil and set aside. Lightly coat a 9-by-5-inch bread pan with cooking spray and set aside.

3. Add the salt to the dough and, in the bowl, knead it in, continuing to knead for at least 5 minutes. Transfer the bread dough to the prepared bowl, turning to coat all sides. Re-cover the bowl and set it in a warm place for at least 3 hours, but it could need up to 4 hours. This is a heavy bread and it may rise, at most, by half and it could be as little as one-fourth.

4. Flour a breadboard or clean work surface and turn the dough out on to it. If necessary, punch the dough down if it is too high. Shape the dough into a rectangle. The short end should be a little shorter than the length of the bread pan. Roll up the dough starting from the short end and place it into the prepared pan, seam-side down.

5. Lightly coat a piece of plastic wrap with olive oil and cover the bread pan with it. Refrigerate overnight.

6. First thing in the morning, remove the bread dough from the refrigerator.

7. In a small bowl, lightly beat the egg (if using). Brush part of the egg over the top of the loaf. Sprinkle the top of the loaf with sesame seeds (if using) and, using a bread lame or very sharp knife, slash the top of the bread dough.

8. Preheat the oven to 400°F.

9. Bake the bread for 30 to 35 minutes, or until it reaches an internal temperature of 200°F on a digital food thermometer.

10. Cool the bread in the pan for 5 minutes before transferring the loaf to a wire rack to cool completely before slicing.

Tip: This loaf could easily be the star of your breakfast table. Slather a warm slice with almond butter and you've got plenty of protein to get you through the day

Rustic Oatmeal Honey Bread

This bread is a bit different than typical rustic breads. The oats make it a heavier bread with fewer holes. The texture is softer as well. You'll also notice that the bread doesn't rise as high as other sourdough doughs after the proofing periods. ***Makes 2 loaves***

FOR ACTIVATING THE STARTER

9½ ounces (1 cup) sourdough starter

4 ounces (½ cup) lukewarm (90°F to 100°F) pure filtered or bottled water

4 ounces (1 cup) whole-wheat flour

FOR THE BREAD DOUGH

12¾ ounces (3 cups) unbleached bread flour, plus more for dusting

19 ounces (2 cups) active sourdough starter

4¾ ounces (1½ cups) old-fashioned rolled oats

8 ounces (1 cup) lukewarm (90°F to 100°F) milk (whole or 2 percent)

3 tablespoons local raw honey

2 tablespoons butter, melted and cooled

1½ teaspoons fine sea salt

Olive oil or nonstick cooking spray, for preparing the bowl and pans

PRE-PREP TIME: 6 TO 12 HOURS TO ACTIVATE THE STARTER

SUGGESTED STARTER: WHOLE WHEAT

SOURDOUGH METHOD: AMBIENT

PREP TIME: 4 HOURS

BAKING TIME: 55 MINUTES

TOTAL TIME: 4 HOURS 55 MINUTES

 *Tools needed*

stand mixer, two 8½-by-4½-inch bread pans

To activate the starter

At least 6 to 12 hours before making the dough, in a medium bowl, combine the starter, lukewarm water, and flour, completely incorporating the ingredients into the starter. Loosely cover and let sit on the counter until ready to use.

To make the bread dough

1. In the bowl of a stand mixer fitted with the dough hook, or a large bowl, stir together the flour, active starter, oats, milk, honey, and butter. Once completely combined, cover the dough with a clean kitchen towel and let rest for at least 20 minutes.

2. Add the salt. Knead the salt into the dough on low speed for at least 5 minutes, or by hand, kneading for 10 minutes. The dough will be sticky. Do not add too much flour, as it will make the bread too stiff and/or dry.

3. Coat another large bowl with olive oil and transfer the bread dough to it, turning to coat all sides. Cover the bowl with a clean kitchen towel and let rise in a warm, draft-free place for 2 hours.

4. Lightly coat two 8½-by-4½-inch bread pans with cooking spray and set aside.

5. Lightly flour a breadboard or clean work surface and turn the dough out on to it. Divide the dough in half. Shape each half into a loaf by pressing the dough into a rectangle. The width of the rectangle should be slightly shorter than the length of the bread pans. Roll up each dough piece from the short edge and place it into the bread pan, seam-side down.

6. Cover the bread pans with a clean kitchen towel and let rise for 90 minutes.

7. Preheat the oven to 375°F.

8. Bake the loaves for 50 to 55 minutes, or until they reach an internal temperature of at least 200°F on a digital food thermometer.

Serving tip: The great thing about this bread is how it tastes after being toasted. To make it taste even better, spread it with peanut butter. It is the ideal breakfast or afternoon snack when served with a big glass of milk or a cup of hot coffee or tea.

Pressure Cooker Artisan Sourdough Bread

This recipe offers a different, quicker way to proof sourdough bread. What better way to keep your bread dough out of a draft and at an even temperature than in a pressure cooker? ***Makes 1 loaf***

FOR ACTIVATING THE STARTER

4¾ ounces (½ cup) sourdough starter

4 ounces (½ cup) lukewarm (90°F to 100°F) pure filtered or bottled water

4 ounces (1 cup) whole-wheat flour, or flour of choice

FOR THE BREAD DOUGH

12¾ ounces (3 cups) unbleached all-purpose flour, plus more for dusting

2.4 ounces (¼ cup) active sourdough starter

1¼ teaspoons fine sea salt

10½ ounces (1⅓ cups) cool (60°F to 70°F) pure filtered or bottled water

Semolina or cornmeal, for dusting

PRE-PREP TIME: 6 TO 12 HOURS TO ACTIVATE THE STARTER

SUGGESTED STARTER: WHOLE WHEAT, OR FLOUR OF CHOICE

SOURDOUGH METHOD: AMBIENT

PREP TIME: 4 HOURS 30 MINUTES

BAKING TIME: 35 MINUTES

TOTAL TIME: 5 HOURS 5 MINUTES

Tools needed

electric pressure cooker, 6-quart Dutch oven, spray bottle

To activate the starter

At least 6 to 12 hours before making the dough, in a medium bowl, combine the starter, lukewarm water, and flour, completely incorporating the ingredients into the starter. Loosely cover and let sit on the counter until ready to use.

To make the bread dough

1. In a large bowl stir together the flour, active starter, salt, and cool water until well combined. The dough will be a little sticky. Form it into a ball.

2. Line your pressure cooker with parchment paper. Place the dough inside on the parchment. Cover the pressure cooker with its lid. Press the Yogurt button. Set the time for 4 hours.

3. Lightly flour a breadboard or clean work surface. Remove the lid from the pressure cooker and carefully remove the parchment with the dough on it. Place the dough on the prepared surface.

4. Lightly flour the top of the dough and your hands. Knead the dough a few times and then shape it into a ball. Keep tucking the edges of the dough underneath while forming the ball.

5. Discard the first piece of parchment paper. Lightly dust a clean piece of parchment with semolina and place the dough on it. Sprinkle the top of the dough with flour and spread it evenly with your hands. Using a bread lame or very sharp knife, cut an X, or other shape, into the top of the dough.

6. Preheat the oven to 450°F. Place a Dutch oven, with its lid on, on the middle rack and heat for 30 minutes.

7. Using oven gloves, pull out the rack the Dutch oven is on. Remove the lid and place it on the stovetop. Using the corners of the parchment paper, transfer the dough and parchment into the hot pot. Spray the bread with water a couple of times, re-cover the pot, and return it to the oven.

8. Reduce the oven temperature to 400°F. Bake the bread, covered, for 25 minutes. Remove the cover and bake for 10 minutes more, or until it reaches an internal temperature of 205°F on a digital food thermometer.

9. Transfer the pan to a wire rack and let the bread cool in the pot for 10 minutes before transferring it to a wire rack to cool completely before slicing.

Tip: If you just can't wait to slice this warm bread, be sure to use an electric knife. Just remember, if the bread is too hot, the interior will be gummy.

Irish Sourdough Bread

Potatoes aren't added to this bread for the taste but rather because they help the bread rise faster. Plus, they also make the bread lighter and moister. Best of all, this bread will last longer than most breads. ***Makes 1 loaf***

FOR ACTIVATING THE STARTER
9½ ounces (1 cup) sourdough starter

4 ounces (½ cup) lukewarm (90°F to 100°F) pure filtered or bottled water

4 ounces (1 cup) whole-wheat flour

FOR THE MASHED POTATOES
6 ounces (¾ cup) water

1 tablespoon butter

¼ teaspoon salt

2.6 ounces (⅓ cup) slightly warm milk

5.2 ounces (⅔ cup) instant mashed potato flakes

FOR THE BREAD DOUGH
5.2 ounces (⅔ cup) room temperature (75°F) pure filtered or bottled water

19 ounces (2 cups) active sourdough starter

12¾ ounces (3 cups) unbleached bread flour, plus more as needed

10 ounces (2½ cups) whole-grain whole-wheat flour

1 teaspoon fine sea salt

Olive oil or nonstick cooking spray, for preparing the bowl

1 cup ice cubes

PRE-PREP TIME: 6 TO 12 HOURS TO ACTIVATE THE STARTER

SUGGESTED STARTER: WHOLE WHEAT

SOURDOUGH METHOD: AMBIENT

PREP TIME: 3 HOURS 36 MINUTES

BAKING TIME: 40 MINUTES

TOTAL TIME: 4 HOURS 16 MINUTES

Tools needed

stand mixer, large rimmed sheet pan, baking stone

To activate the starter
At least 6 to 12 hours before making the dough, in a medium bowl, combine the starter, lukewarm water, and flour, completely incorporating the ingredients into the starter. Loosely cover and let sit on the counter until ready to use.

To make the mashed potatoes
In a small pot over medium-high heat, combine the water, butter, and salt and bring to a boil. Remove the pot from the heat and stir in the milk and potato flakes. Set aside to cool to room temperature (75°F).

To make the bread dough
1. In the bowl of a stand mixer fitted with the paddle attachment, or a large bowl, combine the cooled mashed potatoes, room temperature water, and active starter. Mix on low speed, or by hand, until blended. With the machine still running, or stirring, gradually add the bread flour and whole-grain flour. Change to the dough hook and knead on low speed for 2 minutes, or 4 minutes by hand. If the dough is extremely sticky, add a little more bread flour. Let the dough rest for 20 minutes.

2. Add the salt and knead it in on low speed for 4 minutes, or 8 minutes by hand.

3. Lightly coat another large bowl with olive oil and transfer the dough to it, turning to coat all sides. Cover the bowl loosely with a clean kitchen towel and let rise in a warm, draft-free place for 2 hours.

4. Lightly flour a square piece of parchment paper and turn the dough out on to it. Continually tuck the edges of the dough underneath until a ball forms and the top is taut. Flour a kitchen towel, cover the dough ball with it, and let rise for 1 hour more.

5. Place a large rimmed sheet pan on the bottom rack of your oven and place a baking stone on the rack above it, making sure the pan is large enough to extend out farther on one side of the stone. Preheat the oven to 425°F for 15 minutes.

6. Using a bread lame or very sharp knife, slash the top of the bread dough.

7. Reduce the oven temperature to 400°F. Using the corners of the parchment, transfer the bread to the baking stone.

8. Quickly and carefully put the ice in the pan below the baking stone (do not get any on the stone, as it may crack or break). Quickly close the oven door to allow the ice to melt and, almost immediately, turn to steam.

9. Bake the bread for 40 minutes, or until it reaches an internal temperature of 205°F on a digital food thermometer.

10. Let the bread cool completely before slicing.

Tip: If you don't have a stand mixer, mix the dough with a stiff spatula, a dough scraper, or by hand. Instead of adding additional flour to alleviate the sticky dough, knead it a bit longer.

Chapter Four
ENRICHED FLOURS, WHOLE GRAINS, AND SPECIALTY BREADS

Many of us are interested in eating healthier by getting back to whole foods. A good portion of these foods contain natural grains such as whole wheat, berry, and other specialty flours. Other desirable ingredients in a whole-food diet are nuts and seeds. Nuts and seeds add necessary proteins to our diets. This chapter presents sourdough bread recipes made with ingredients such as spelt, rye flour, pumpernickel flour, flaxseed, quinoa, chia seeds, fruits, and nuts.

Honey Spelt Bread

Spelt is a nutty wheat with more nutrients than regular wheats. It's known to be a good source of dietary fiber, protein, and vitamins. Spelt is also easier to digest. This is another bread that makes a wonderful breakfast or afternoon snack. It tastes good either at room temperature or warm. If you want to grab a piece of bread for a snack, this is the best one to choose. ***Makes 2 loaves***

FOR ACTIVATING THE STARTER

4¾ ounces (½ cup) sourdough starter

4 ounces (½ cup) lukewarm (90°F to 100°F) pure filtered or bottled water

4 ounces (heaping 1 cup) rye flour or (1 cup) whole-wheat flour

FOR THE BREAD DOUGH

1½ teaspoons dry yeast

12 ounces (1½ cups) warm (100°F to 125°F) pure filtered or bottled water

9½ ounces (1 cup) active sourdough starter

1 tablespoon honey

8½ ounces (2 cups) unbleached bread flour, plus more for dusting

5 ounces (1¼ cups) spelt flour

4 ounces (1 cup) whole-grain whole-wheat flour

1 tablespoon fine sea salt

Olive oil or nonstick cooking spray, for preparing the bowl and pans

PRE-PREP TIME: 6 TO 12 HOURS TO ACTIVATE THE STARTER

SUGGESTED STARTER: RYE OR WHOLE WHEAT

SOURDOUGH METHOD: RETARDED

PREP TIME: 1 HOUR 15 MINUTES

BAKING TIME: 45 MINUTES

TOTAL TIME: 2 HOURS

 *Tools needed*

stand mixer, two 9-by-5-inch bread pans

To activate the starter

At least 6 to 12 hours before making the dough, in a medium bowl, combine the starter, lukewarm water, and flour, completely incorporating the ingredients into the starter. Loosely cover and let sit on the counter until ready to use.

To make the bread dough

1. In the bowl of a stand mixer, or a large bowl, stir together the yeast and warm water. Add the active starter and honey and stir to combine completely. Let sit for 5 minutes to proof the yeast.

2. Attach the dough hook to the mixer and add the bread flour, spelt flour, whole-wheat flour, and salt. Mix on low speed, or by hand, until all the ingredients are combined.

3. Flour a breadboard or clean work surface and turn the dough out on to it. Knead the dough until it is no longer sticky, about 5 minutes, adding more flour as needed, but not so much that the dough is no longer soft. Knead for 1 to 2 minutes more, if needed. Shape the dough into a ball.

4. Coat a large bowl with olive oil and transfer the dough to it, turning to coat all sides.

5. Cover the bowl with plastic wrap. Place the bowl in the oven with the light on. Do not turn on the oven. Let the dough rise for 1½ hours, or longer if necessary, until the dough doubles in size.

6. Coat two 9-by-5-inch bread pans with cooking spray and set aside.

7. Flour a breadboard or clean work surface. Divide the dough in half and place it on the prepared surface. Press each half into a rectangle with a width slightly less than the length of the bread pans. Roll up the dough rectangles from the short sides and place them, seam-side down, into the prepared pans.

8. Lightly coat two pieces of plastic wrap with olive oil and cover the pans with them. Place the pans in a warm, draft-free area to rise for 45 minutes.

9. Preheat the oven to 450°F.

10. Remove the plastic wrap from the bread. Sprinkle flour over the top of each loaf and spread it evenly with your hands. Using a bread lame or very sharp knife, cut diagonal lines into the dough. Don't be afraid to cut deep.

11. Put the bread pans into the oven. Reduce the oven temperature to 400°F. Bake for 40 to 45 minutes until the crust is dark golden brown and the loaves reach an internal temperature of 200°F on a digital food thermometer.

12. Let the bread cool in the pans for 10 minutes, before transferring them to a wire rack to cool completely before slicing.

Tip: Only have whole-wheat starter, but you want to cultivate a rye one, too? Feed 2 tablespoons of your original starter with equal parts rye flour and water. Do this for a week and you've got a rye starter. Just remember to save some of your original starter, as you won't want to make only rye breads from now on.

Rye Bread Rolls with Caraway Seeds

You could make rye bread using all rye flour, but it would be a dense bread. This recipe lightens things up by adding bread flour to the rye starter, rye flour combination. Rye by itself imparts a slightly sour taste, which intensifies when using a sourdough starter. ***Makes 6 rolls***

FOR ACTIVATING THE STARTER

4¾ ounces (½ cup) sourdough starter

2 ounces (¼ cup) lukewarm (90°F to 100°F) pure filtered or bottled water

2 ounces (heaping ½ cup) rye flour

FOR THE BREAD DOUGH

3 ounces (⅓ cup) active rye sourdough starter

10 ounces (1¼ cups) room temperature (75°F) pure filtered or bottled water

7½ ounces (1¾ cups) unbleached bread flour, plus more for dusting

6⅓ ounces (1¾ cups) rye flour

1 tablespoon caraway seeds

1 teaspoon fine sea salt

1 cup ice cubes

PRE-PREP TIME: 6 TO 12 HOURS TO ACTIVATE THE STARTER

SUGGESTED STARTER: RYE

SOURDOUGH METHOD: AMBIENT

PREP TIME: 45 MINUTES, PLUS OVERNIGHT IN THE REFRIGERATOR

BAKING TIME: 15 TO 20 MINUTES

TOTAL TIME: ABOUT 1 HOUR, PLUS OVERNIGHT IN THE REFRIGERATOR

Tools needed

baking stone, large rimmed sheet pan

To activate the starter

At least 6 to 12 hours before making the dough, in a medium bowl, combine the starter, lukewarm water, and flour, completely incorporating the ingredients into the starter. Loosely cover and let sit on the counter until ready to use.

To make the bread dough

1. In a large bowl, combine the active starter and room temperature water. Stir until well combined. Add the bread flour, rye flour, and caraway seeds and stir to combine. Cover the bowl with a clean kitchen towel and let rest for 20 minutes.

2. Add the salt and, in the bowl, knead it in. Re-cover the bowl and let rest for 20 minutes more. Knead the dough, in the bowl, for 5 minutes. Cover the bowl with plastic wrap and let sit overnight, or for at least 12 hours.

3. Flour a breadboard or clean work surface and turn the dough out on to it. Knead for 5 minutes. Weigh the dough and divide the weight by six. Divide the dough into six equal parts, by weight.

4. On the floured surface, roll each piece of dough into a ball. Flour a clean kitchen towel and cover the dough balls with it. Let rest for 20 minutes.

5. Place a large rimmed sheet pan on the bottom rack of your oven and place a baking stone on the rack above it, making sure the pan is large enough to extend out farther on one side of the stone. Preheat the oven to 450°F.

6. Using a bread lame or very sharp knife, slash the tops of the rolls and carefully place them on the heated baking stone.

7. Quickly and carefully put the ice in the pan below the baking stone (do not get any on the stone, as it may crack or break). Quickly close the oven door to allow the ice to melt and, almost immediately, turn to steam.

8. Reduce the oven temperature to 410°F and bake the rolls for 15 to 20 minutes until golden brown.

9. Transfer the rolls to a wire rack to cool slightly before serving.

Tip: These rolls are perfect with any meal or make a delightful party snack. Have plenty of good quality butter on hand. Use them for mini sandwiches such as pimiento cheese, which is easy to make: Shred an 8-ounce block of extra-sharp Cheddar cheese and place it in a medium bowl. Drain half the liquid from a 4-ounce jar of sliced—not diced—pimientos and empty the jar into the bowl. Add 1 to 2 tablespoons of good quality mayonnaise, or more if you prefer. Stir together, breaking up the pimientos as you mix the ingredients. Add a dash of hot sauce, if you like. Some people also sprinkle it with a little garlic.

High-Protein Sourdough Bread

Looking to boost your protein, but prefer eating bread over animal protein? This bread is made with quinoa, chia seeds, and flaxseed, which give it a protein boost. Slather a piece with cream cheese and you've upped your protein game even more. ***Makes 1 loaf***

FOR ACTIVATING THE STARTER

2 tablespoons to 2.4 ounces (¼ cup) sourdough starter

2 ounces (¼ cup) lukewarm (90°F to 100°F) pure filtered or bottled water

2 ounces (½ cup) unbleached pumpernickel flour or whole-wheat flour

FOR THE BREAD DOUGH

1.4 ounces (3 tablespoons plus 2 teaspoons) quinoa, rinsed well

1 tablespoon flaxseed

1 tablespoon chia seeds

2½ ounces (⅓ cup) boiling water

3 ounces (⅓ cup) active pumpernickel sourdough starter

12 ounces (1½ cups) room temperature (75°F) pure filtered or bottled water

12¾ ounces (3 cups) unbleached bread flour, plus more for dusting

3.6 ounces (1 cup) rye flour, or 4 ounces (1 cup) whole-wheat flour

2 teaspoons fine sea salt

PRE-PREP TIME: 6 TO 12 HOURS TO ACTIVATE THE STARTER
SUGGESTED STARTER: PUMPERNICKEL OR WHOLE WHEAT
SOURDOUGH METHOD: RETARDED
PREP TIME: 7 HOURS 20 MINUTES, PLUS OVERNIGHT IN THE REFRIGERATOR
BAKING TIME: 40 MINUTES
TOTAL TIME: 8 HOURS, PLUS OVERNIGHT IN THE REFRIGERATOR

Tools needed
6-quart Dutch oven, spray bottle

To activate the starter

At least 6 to 12 hours before making the dough, in a medium bowl, combine the starter, lukewarm water, and flour, completely incorporating the ingredients into the starter. Loosely cover and let sit on the counter until ready to use.

To make the bread dough

1. In a small bowl, stir together the quinoa, flaxseed, and chia seeds. Pour the boiling water over them and set the bowl aside to soak.

2. In a large bowl, combine the active starter, room temperature water, bread flour, and rye flour. Cover the bowl with a clean kitchen towel and let the dough rest for 90 minutes.

3. Add the salt and, in the bowl, knead it in. Re-cover the dough and let rest for 30 minutes more.

4. Using your hands, a rubber spatula, or dough scraper, knead the bread dough, in the bowl, four times. Add the quinoa and seeds and knead them in. Knead a couple more times. Re-cover the bowl and let the dough proof on the counter for 2 to 3 hours until it grows by at least 50 percent.

5. Cover the bowl with plastic wrap and refrigerate overnight.

6. The next day, flour a breadboard or clean surface and turn the dough out on to it. Shape the dough into a round boule and let rest for 20 minutes.

7. Transfer the dough to a square piece of parchment paper and do one final shaping. Cover with a clean kitchen towel and let proof for 1 hour to 90 minutes.

8. Using a bread lame or very sharp knife, slash the top of the dough.

9. Preheat the oven to 450°F. Place a Dutch oven, with its lid on, in the oven for 30 minutes.

10. Using oven gloves, pull out the rack the Dutch oven is on. Remove the lid and place it on the stovetop. Using the corners of the parchment, transfer the bread dough and parchment into the hot pot. Spray the bread with water a couple of times, re-cover the pot, and return it to the oven. Reduce the oven temperature to 425°F. Bake for 25 minutes.

11. Remove the lid and continue baking for 15 minutes more, or until the crust is golden brown and the loaf reaches an internal temperature of 200°F on a digital food thermometer.

Tip: Pumpernickel flour is a darker version of rye than regular rye flour. It is also a bit more tart than a regular rye flour and definitely more tart than a typical whole-wheat starter.

Black Pumpernickel Bread

This bread gets its dark color and complex flavor profile from pumpernickel rye flour, coffee, molasses, and cocoa. ***Makes 2 loaves***

FOR ACTIVATING THE STARTER

9½ ounces (1 cup) whole-wheat sourdough starter

10½ ounces (1⅓ cups) strong black coffee (75°F to 80°F)

8 ounces (2 cups) pumpernickel flour

FOR THE BREAD DOUGH

8½ ounces (2 cups) unbleached bread flour, plus more as needed

3.6 ounces (1 cup) rye or (4 ounces) pumpernickel flour

1 ounce (¼ cup) unsweetened cocoa powder

4 ounces (½ cup) lukewarm (90°F to 100°F) pure filtered or bottled water

3 ounces (¼ cup) molasses

1½ teaspoons fine sea salt

Olive oil or nonstick cooking spray, for preparing the bowl

2 cups ice cubes

PRE-PREP TIME: 6 TO 12 HOURS TO ACTIVATE THE STARTER
SUGGESTED STARTER: WHOLE-WHEAT MADE INTO PUMPERNICKEL
SOURDOUGH METHOD: RETARDED
PREP TIME: 45 MINUTES, PLUS OVERNIGHT IN THE REFRIGERATOR
BAKING TIME: 50 MINUTES
TOTAL TIME: 1 HOUR 35 MINUTES, PLUS OVERNIGHT IN THE REFRIGERATOR

Tools needed

baking stone, bread lame or very sharp knife, large rimmed sheet pan

To activate the starter

At least 6 to 12 hours before starting the bread dough, in a large bowl, combine the starter, coffee, and flour, completely incorporating the ingredients into the starter. Loosely cover and let sit on the counter until ready to use.

To make the bread dough

1. In a large bowl, combine the entire amount of activated starter, bread flour, rye flour, cocoa powder, lukewarm water, and molasses. Mix completely. Cover the bowl with a clean kitchen towel and let rest for 20 minutes.

2. Add the salt and, in the bowl, knead it in, continuing to knead for 5 minutes or so. If the dough is really sticky, add a bit more flour, but not too much or you'll dry out the bread dough.

3. Coat a large bowl with olive oil and transfer the dough to it, turning to coat all sides. Cover the dough with plastic wrap and refrigerate overnight.

4. Remove the dough from the refrigerator and let it sit on the counter to warm a little.

5. Turn the dough out onto a floured work surface. De-gas (press down on) the dough a few times if it has risen too much.

6. Divide the dough in half and stretch each piece to a foot or so in length. Working with one piece, fold one short end about three-fourths of the way toward the other short end. Fold the other end in the same manner. Starting at the long side of the dough, roll it toward the other long end. Tuck the ends under and then roll, flat-handed, until the loaf is even and smooth. Repeat this with the other piece of dough. Flour the tops of the loaves and cover them with a kitchen towel. Let proof for 20 minutes.

7. Place a large rimmed sheet pan on the bottom rack of your oven and place a baking stone on the rack above it, making sure the pan is large enough to extend out farther on one side of the stone. Preheat the oven to 450°F.

8. Place the loaves on a large piece of parchment paper. Using a bread lame or very sharp knife, slash each loaf diagonally. Carefully place the loaves and the parchment onto the baking stone.

9. Quickly and carefully put the ice in the pan below the baking stone (do not get any on the stone, as it may crack or break). Quickly close the oven door to allow the ice to melt and, almost immediately, turn to steam. Bake for 20 minutes.

10. Using oven gloves, rotate the piece of parchment with the bread on it 180 degrees (front to back). Bake for 30 minutes more.

11. Remove the bread from the oven and cool completely on wire racks.

Tip: Try dipping pumpernickel bread in a Swiss cheese fondue. In a medium bowl, toss together 2 cups of shredded Swiss cheese and 2 tablespoons of cornstarch. Rub ½ garlic clove around the inside of a medium saucepan over medium-high heat. Throw the garlic away. Add 2 cups of white wine to the pot and bring to a simmer. Stir in the cheese; reduce the heat to low, and cook until completely melted and bubbly. Just before serving add a couple grinds of black pepper and a sprinkling of freshly grated nutmeg.

Whole-Wheat Sourdough Rolls

Looking for the ideal dinner roll recipe? Here it is. I like to serve mine in a basket lined with a fine dinner napkin. Just have plenty of room temperature butter on hand for spreading on these delicious rolls. ***Makes 24 rolls***

FOR ACTIVATING THE STARTER

2 tablespoons to 2.4 ounces (¼ cup) sourdough starter

2 ounces (¼ cup) lukewarm (90°F to 100°F) pure filtered or bottled water

2 ounces (½ cup) whole-wheat flour

FOR THE BREAD DOUGH

4¾ ounces (½ cup) active whole-wheat sourdough starter

18 ounces (2¼ cups) cool (60°F to 70°F) pure filtered or bottled water

1½ teaspoons fine sea salt

2 ounces (¼ cup) butter, at room temperature, divided, plus more for preparing the baking dish

3 ounces (¼ cup) pure maple syrup, or honey

24 ounces (6 cups) whole-wheat flour, plus more as needed

PRE-PREP TIME: 6 TO 12 HOURS TO ACTIVATE THE STARTER
SUGGESTED STARTER: WHOLE WHEAT
SOURDOUGH METHOD: AMBIENT
PREP TIME: 8 HOURS 10 MINUTES
BAKING TIME: 25 TO 30 MINUTES
TOTAL TIME: 8 HOURS 40 MINUTES

Tools needed

stand mixer, 9-by-13-inch baking pan, bread lame or very sharp knife

To activate the starter

At least 6 to 12 hours before making the dough, in a medium bowl, combine the starter, lukewarm water, and flour, completely incorporating the ingredients into the starter. Loosely cover and let sit on the counter until ready to use.

To make the bread dough

1. Early in the morning, in the bowl of a stand mixer fitted with the paddle attachment, or in a large bowl and using a handheld electric mixer, combine the active starter, water, salt, 2 tablespoons of butter, the maple syrup, and whole-wheat flour. Mix on low speed until the ingredients are fully combined, adding more flour if the dough is too sticky, but not more than 4 ounces (1 cup, or 7 cups total).

2. Attach the dough hook and knead on low speed for at least 10 minutes, or 15 to 20 minutes by hand.

3. Cover the bowl with a piece of plastic wrap and let the dough rest for 6 hours.

4. Coat a 9-by-13-inch baking pan with butter. Evenly divide the dough into 24 pieces. Flour a breadboard or clean work surface and, on it, shape each piece into a ball with a slightly open hand, rolling the dough in a circular motion until you get a tight surface. Place the rolls in the prepared pan. Flour a kitchen towel and cover the rolls with it. Let rise for 2 hours.

5. Preheat the oven to 375°F.

6. Using a bread lame or very sharp knife, mark each roll with an X. Melt the remaining 2 tablespoons of butter.

7. Bake the rolls for 25 to 30 minutes, or until brown. Remove from the oven and brush the rolls with melted butter before serving.

Tip: The most precise way to divide this dough is to weigh it first. Divide that amount by 24 and then weigh each piece so it equals that amount.

Artisan Apple Bread

This Artisan Apple Bread is perfect when you need just a little something sweet. Serve it sliced with a good quality honey or cream cheese. It's perfect with a cup of tea. This bread would also work on a platter with more apples, a few grapes, and various flavors of cheese—both sharp and mild. ***Makes 1 loaf***

FOR ACTIVATING THE STARTER

2 tablespoons to 2.4 ounces (¼ cup) sourdough starter

2 ounces (¼ cup) lukewarm (90°F to 100°F) pure filtered or bottled water

2 ounces (½ cup) whole-wheat flour

FOR THE BREAD DOUGH

Nonstick cooking spray, for preparing the baking pan

1 medium sweet-tart apple (Gala, Honeycrisp, etc.), washed, peeled, and finely chopped

½ teaspoon ground cinnamon

½ teaspoon ground nutmeg

2.4 ounces (¼ cup) active sourdough starter

12 ounces (1½ cups) room temperature (75°F) pure filtered or bottled water

15 ounces (3½ cups) unbleached bread flour, plus more for dusting

2 ounces (½ cup) spelt flour

1½ teaspoons fine sea salt

PRE-PREP TIME: 6 TO 12 HOURS TO ACTIVATE THE STARTER, PLUS APPLE ROASTING

SUGGESTED STARTER: WHOLE WHEAT

SOURDOUGH METHOD: AMBIENT

PREP TIME: 9 HOURS

BAKING TIME: 40 MINUTES

TOTAL TIME: 9 HOURS 40 MINUTES

Tools needed

square baking pan, 6-quart Dutch oven, bread lame or very sharp knife, spray bottle

To activate the starter

At least 6 to 12 hours before making the dough, in a medium bowl, combine the starter, lukewarm water, and flour, completely incorporating the ingredients into the starter. Loosely cover and let sit on the counter until ready to use.

To make the bread dough

1. Preheat the oven to 400°F. Line a square baking pan with aluminum foil and lightly coat it with cooking spray.

2. In a small bowl, toss together the apple, cinnamon, and nutmeg. Transfer the apples to the prepared pan and bake for 30 minutes, tossing at least once during baking. Remove and set aside. Turn off the oven.

3. In a large bowl, stir together the active starter, water, bread flour, and spelt flour until combined. Cover the bowl with a clean kitchen towel and let rest for 30 minutes and up to 1 hour.

4. Add the salt and, in the bowl, knead it in by folding the dough over and pushing on it. Continue kneading until a

smooth ball forms. The dough will begin to tighten. Spread the dough out a bit and knead in the apple pieces, evenly distributing them, without crushing.

5. Cover the dough with a clean damp towel and let rest at room temperature (75°F) until doubled in size, about 8 hours.

6. Lightly flour a breadboard or clean work surface and turn the dough out on to it. Using floured hands, form the dough into a round shape by continually tucking the edges under as you turn the ball.

7. Flour a clean kitchen towel and line a small bowl with it, or flour a banneton basket and place the dough in it, seam-side up. Cover the dough with another floured kitchen towel. Let rise for 30 minutes to 1 hour.

8. Preheat the oven to 450°F. Place your Dutch oven, with its lid on, in the oven.

9. Cut a square of parchment paper and place it over the top of the dough. Carefully flip the bread dough onto the parchment. Sprinkle a little more flour over the top of the dough. Spread it evenly with your hands. Using a bread lame or very sharp knife, cut an X, or some other design, into the dough.

10. Reduce the oven temperature to 425°F. Using oven gloves, pull out the oven rack with the Dutch oven on it. Remove the lid and place it on the stovetop. Using the corners of the parchment, transfer the dough and parchment into the hot pot. Spray the bread with water a couple of times and re-cover the pot. Bake for 30 minutes.

11. Using oven gloves, remove the lid and bake for 10 minutes more, until the top is golden brown and the loaf sounds hollow when thumped.

Tip: If you prefer sweet-tart apples, try Gala, Pink Lady, or Honeycrisp apples. If you prefer a tarter apple, try Granny Smith apples.

Sourdough Marble Rye Bread

What a delight it is to cut a slice of this marble rye and see the dark- and light-colored swirls. I like to have the dark on the outside and the light on the inside, but you can do it the other way just by placing the lighter dough on the bottom. ***Makes 1 loaf***

FOR ACTIVATING THE STARTER

2 tablespoons to 2.4 ounces (¼ cup) sourdough starter

2 ounces (¼ cup) lukewarm (90°F to 100°F) pure filtered or bottled water

2 ounces (heaping ½ cup) rye flour

FOR THE BREAD DOUGH

3 ounces (⅓ cup) active rye sourdough starter

10 ounces (1¼ cups) room temperature (75°F) pure filtered or bottled water

7½ ounces (1¾ cups) unbleached bread flour, plus more for dusting

1¼ teaspoons fine sea salt

3.4 ounces (scant 1 cup) rye flour

3.4 ounces (heaping ¾ cup) pumpernickel flour

Nonstick cooking spray, for preparing the bread pan

PRE-PREP TIME: 6 TO 12 HOURS TO ACTIVATE THE STARTER

SUGGESTED STARTER: RYE

SOURDOUGH METHOD: RETARDED

PREP TIME: 45 MINUTES, PLUS 12 HOURS FOR OVERNIGHT REST

BAKING TIME: 40 MINUTES

TOTAL TIME: 1 HOUR 25 MINUTES, PLUS 12 HOURS FOR OVERNIGHT REST

Tools needed
9-by-5-inch bread pan

To activate the starter

At least 6 to 12 hours before making the dough, in a medium bowl, combine the starter, lukewarm water, and flour, completely incorporating the ingredients into the starter. Loosely cover and let sit on the counter until ready to use.

To make the bread dough

1. In a large bowl, stir together the active starter and room temperature water until well mixed. Stir in the bread flour and salt. Divide the dough in half and place each half in a large bowl. Stir the rye flour into one bowl and the pumpernickel flour into the other. Cover the bowls with clean kitchen towels and let sit for 20 minutes.

2. Knead the doughs, in the bowls, for 5 minutes each. Cover the bowls with plastic wrap and let sit overnight, or for at least 12 hours.

3. Lightly flour a breadboard or clean work surface and turn the pumpernickel dough out on to it. Knead for 5 minutes.

4. Remove the rye flour dough from its bowl and place it on the prepared surface. Knead for 5 minutes.

5. Pat out the pumpernickel dough into a rectangle no wider than the length of the bread pan. Press the rye dough into a rectangle of similar size. Cover each piece of dough with a clean floured kitchen towel. Let rest for 20 minutes.

6. Lightly coat a 9-by-5-inch bread pan with cooking spray.

7. Place the rye dough on top of the pumpernickel dough. Starting at the short end of the dough, roll the two doughs together. Place the bread dough into the prepared pan. Re-cover the bread dough with the floured towel and set aside for 10 minutes while the oven preheats.

8. Preheat the oven to 450°F.

9. Bake the marble rye for 40 minutes until the top is crusty and the loaf sounds hollow when thumped. Transfer the bread to a wire rack to cool.

Tip: This is another sourdough bread that just cries, "Toast me and spread me with peanut butter for breakfast." In these days of healthier eating habits, spreading the toast with fresh avocado is tasty, too. Another favorite sandwich using this Sourdough Marble Rye is grilled cheese. Use real butter on the bread along with a very sharp white Cheddar cheese. Some people add bacon or ham before grilling.

Six-Grain Sourdough Bread Boule

This six-grain bread is one of those recipes with many options. You could make it with just about any starter flavor you choose. Just keep in mind that different starters may need a bit more water or flour, and they may take less or more time to bake. The other option is to mix and match the grains, too. Once again, baking times and water and flour needs may vary. ***Makes 1 round boule***

FOR ACTIVATING THE STARTER

2 tablespoons to ¼ cup (2.4 ounces) sourdough starter

2 ounces (¼ cup) lukewarm (90°F to 100°F) pure filtered or bottled water

2 ounces (½ cup) whole-wheat flour, pumpernickel flour, or (heaping ½ cup) rye flour

FOR THE GRAINS

1¾ ounces (¼ cup) pearl barley

2 tablespoons buckwheat

2 tablespoons quinoa, rinsed well

2 tablespoons steel cut oats

2 tablespoons sunflower seeds

1 tablespoon pumpkin seeds

6 ounces (¾ cup) room temperature (75°F) pure filtered or bottled water

FOR THE BREAD DOUGH

2.4 ounces (¼ cup) active whole-wheat sourdough starter

10½ ounces (1⅓ cups) room temperature (75°F) pure filtered or bottled water

2½ tablespoons honey, preferably local, or pure maple syrup

8 ounces (2 cups) whole-grain whole-wheat bread flour

6½ ounces (1½ cups) unbleached bread flour, plus more for dusting

1½ teaspoons fine sea salt

Olive oil or nonstick cooking spray, for preparing the bowl

PRE-PREP TIME: 6 TO 12 HOURS TO ACTIVATE THE STARTER, PLUS OVERNIGHT FOR THE GRAIN SOAK

SUGGESTED STARTER: WHOLE WHEAT, PUMPERNICKEL, RYE, ETC.

SOURDOUGH METHOD: RETARDED

PREP TIME: 6 HOURS 25 MINUTES, PLUS OVERNIGHT IN THE REFRIGERATOR

BAKING TIME: 55 MINUTES

TOTAL TIME: 7 HOURS 20 MINUTES, PLUS OVERNIGHT IN THE REFRIGERATOR

Tools needed

6-quart Dutch oven, bread lame or very sharp knife, spray bottle

To activate the starter

At least 6 to 12 hours before making the dough, in a medium bowl, combine the starter, lukewarm water, and flour, completely incorporating the ingredients into the starter. Loosely cover and let sit on the counter until ready to use.

To prepare the grains

The afternoon before making the bread, in a small bowl, combine the barley, buckwheat, quinoa, oats, sunflower and pumpkin seeds, and water. Let soak overnight. Drain, if needed.

To make the bread dough

1. The next day, in a large bowl, stir together the soaked seeds, active starter, room temperature water, and honey. Add the whole-wheat flour and bread flour and stir to combine. Let rest for 20 minutes.

2. Add the salt and, in the bowl, knead it in, continuing to knead for at least 5 minutes more. If kneading is difficult, fold the dough over from one side to the other and then top to bottom.

3. Coat a large bowl with olive oil and transfer the dough to it, turning to coat all sides. Cover the bowl with a clean kitchen towel and place in a warm place for 3 to 4 hours. At least twice during this time, knead or fold the bread dough.

4. Cover the bowl with plastic wrap and refrigerate overnight.

5. The next morning, flour a breadboard or clean work surface and turn the dough out on to it. Form the dough into a round shape by continually tucking the edges of the dough under as you turn the ball until the top is tight.

6. Generously flour a proofing basket and place the dough ball, seam-side up, in it. If you don't have a basket, place the dough, seam-side down, inside a Dutch oven lined with parchment paper. Let the dough rise for 1 to 2 hours more.

7. Preheat the oven to 475°F.

8. Using a bread lame or very sharp knife, cut an X into the top of the loaf. Don't be afraid to cut down into the loaf. Transfer the loaf to a Dutch oven, if it's in a proofing basket. Spray the bread with water a couple of times and place the lid on the pot. Place the pot in the oven and reduce the oven temperature to 450°F. Bake for 20 minutes.

9. Remove the lid and bake for 30 to 35 minutes more until the top is golden brown and the loaf sounds hollow when thumped.

10. Let the bread cool in the pot for 5 minutes before transferring it to a wire rack to cool completely before slicing.

Sourdough Baguettes

Although this recipe is called Sourdough Baguettes, the directions are for sourdough batons, which are smaller versions of the traditional 2-foot-long baguettes. Not everyone's oven can handle baguettes, but most can handle a 1-foot-long baton. **Makes 4 batons**

FOR ACTIVATING THE STARTER

4¾ ounces (½ cup) sourdough starter

4 ounces (½ cup) lukewarm (90°F to 100°F) pure filtered or bottled water

4 ounces (1 cup) whole-wheat flour, or flour of choice

FOR THE BATON DOUGH

9½ ounces (1 cup) active sourdough starter

13 ounces (3 cups) unbleached bread flour, plus more for dusting

4 ounces (1 cup) whole-grain whole-wheat flour

10½ ounces (1⅓ cups) room temperature (75°F) pure filtered or bottled water

2 teaspoons fine sea salt

1 cup ice cubes

PRE-PREP TIME: 6 TO 12 HOURS TO ACTIVATE THE STARTER
SUGGESTED STARTER: WHOLE WHEAT, OR FLOUR OF CHOICE
SOURDOUGH METHOD: RETARDED
PREP TIME: 3 HOURS 10 MINUTES, PLUS OVERNIGHT IN THE REFRIGERATOR
BAKING TIME: 25 MINUTES
TOTAL TIME: 3 HOURS 35 MINUTES, PLUS OVERNIGHT IN THE REFRIGERATOR

Tools needed

stand mixer, large rimmed sheet pan, baking stone, flexible dough scraper, bread lame or very sharp knife

To activate the starter

At least 6 to 12 hours before making the dough, in a medium bowl, combine the starter, lukewarm water, and flour, completely incorporating the ingredients into the starter. Loosely cover and let sit on the counter until ready to use.

To make the baton dough

1. In the bowl of a stand mixer, or a large bowl, stir together the active starter, bread flour, whole-wheat flour, and room temperature water until the flour is completely incorporated into the dough. Let sit for 20 minutes.

2. Attach the dough hook. Add the salt and knead the dough on low speed for 5 minutes, or 10 minutes by hand. The dough will be shaggy. Remove the bowl from the machine and use a flexible dough scraper to fold the dough, scraping from the bottom, up and over the top. Turn the bowl and repeat. Continue this process for 5 minutes more.

3. Cover the bowl with a clean kitchen towel and let rest for 1 hour. Repeat the dough scraping and folding for 5 minutes, re-cover, and let rest for 1 hour more.

4. Cover the dough with a piece of plastic, pressing it down onto the top of the dough so it won't dry out. Over the top of the bowl, place another piece of plastic to keep the air out. Refrigerate the dough overnight.

5. Remove the bowl from the refrigerator and put it on the kitchen counter. Remove all the plastic wrap and cover the bowl with a clean kitchen towel. Let sit for 1 hour.

6. Divide the dough into four pieces. Flour a breadboard or clean work surface and put the dough on it. Shape each piece into a log about 1 foot long. Tuck the ends under and then roll, flat-handed, until the loaf is even and smooth all around. Try to make the batons about the same size. Flour the tops of the bread dough loaves and cover with a clean kitchen towel. Let the loaves proof for 30 minutes, or until they double in size.

7. Place a large rimmed sheet pan on the bottom rack of your oven and set a baking stone on the rack above it, making sure the pan is large enough to extend out farther on one side of the stone. Preheat the oven to 450°F.

8. Using a bread lame or very sharp knife, slash each loaf. Line a baking sheet with a piece of parchment paper slightly smaller than the baking stone. Place the loaves on the paper.

9. Using oven gloves, carefully slide the parchment with the batons onto the baking stone.

10. Quickly and carefully put the ice in the pan below the baking stone (do not get any on the stone, as it may crack or break). Quickly close the oven door to allow the ice to melt and, almost immediately, turn to steam. Reduce the oven temperature to 400°F and bake for 25 minutes.

11. Using oven gloves, remove the loaves from the oven. Try not to squeeze the bread. Place the loaves on a wire rack to cool completely.

Cuban Medianoche Sourdough Bread

This bread is not typically made with a sourdough starter. Also unusual is the use of dry yeast. Its addition lessens the proofing time. Make your next homemade Cuban sandwich truly special by using this bread. ***Makes 2 free-form loaves***

FOR ACTIVATING THE STARTER

4¾ ounces (½ cup) sourdough starter

4 ounces (½ cup) lukewarm (90°F to 100°F) pure filtered or bottled water

4 ounces (1 cup) whole-wheat flour

FOR THE BREAD DOUGH

2¼ teaspoons active dry yeast

2 teaspoons sugar

6 ounces (¾ cup) room temperature (75°F) pure filtered or bottled water

3 tablespoons good quality lard, or butter, melted and cooled

2 teaspoons fine sea salt

10.6 ounces (2½ cups) unbleached all-purpose flour, or unbleached bread flour, plus more for dusting

9½ ounces (1 cup) active whole-wheat sourdough starter

Olive oil or nonstick cooking spray, for preparing the bowl

2 cups ice cubes

PRE-PREP TIME: 6 TO 12 HOURS TO ACTIVATE THE STARTER

SUGGESTED STARTER: WHOLE WHEAT

SOURDOUGH METHOD: AMBIENT

PREP TIME: 4 HOURS 15 MINUTES

BAKING TIME: 25 MINUTES

TOTAL TIME: 4 HOURS 40 MINUTES

Tools needed

stand mixer, baking stone, parchment paper, baking pan, bread lame or very sharp knife

To activate the starter

At least 6 to 12 hours before making the dough, in a medium bowl, combine the starter, lukewarm water, and flour, completely incorporating the ingredients into the starter. Loosely cover and let sit on the counter until ready to use.

To make the bread dough

1. In the bowl of a stand mixer, or a large bowl, whisk the yeast and sugar. Add the room temperature water and whisk again. Let sit for at least 15 minutes.

2. Add the lard, salt, flour, and active starter to the bowl. Attach the dough hook and mix together on low speed, or stir by hand with a large wooden spoon.

3. Flour a breadboard or clean work surface and turn the dough out on to it. Knead the dough until it forms a firm ball. Use more flour, if necessary, to keep the dough from being overly sticky. Just don't add too much.

4. Generously coat a large bowl with olive oil and transfer the dough to it, turning to coat all sides. Cover the bowl with plastic wrap and set in a warm place to rise for 2 hours.

5. Flour a breadboard or clean work surface and turn the dough out on to it. Divide the dough in half. Shape the dough into two free-form loaves. Roll one piece into a log about 1 foot long. Tuck the ends under and roll the dough until it's smooth. Repeat with the other loaf. Cover with a clean floured kitchen towel and let the loaves proof for 1½ hours, or until they double in size.

6. Place a large rimmed sheet pan on the bottom rack of your oven and place a baking stone on the rack above it, making sure the pan is large enough to extend out farther on one side of the stone, and preheat the oven to 450°F.

7. Place the bread dough loaves on a large piece of parchment paper. Using a bread lame or very sharp knife, slash each loaf diagonally. Carefully transfer the bread loaves and parchment onto the baking stone.

8. Quickly and carefully put the ice in the pan below the baking stone (do not get any on the stone, as it may crack or break). Quickly close the oven door to allow the ice to melt and, almost immediately, turn to steam. Bake for 10 minutes.

9. Using oven gloves or a couple pairs of tongs, turn the parchment with the bread on it 180 degrees (front to back) and bake for 15 minutes more.

10. Remove the bread from the oven and cool completely on wire racks.

Chapter Five
PAN LOAVES AND SANDWICH BREADS

We owe a big thanks to the fourth Earl of Sandwich. If he hadn't wanted to hold his entire meal between two pieces of bread, we wouldn't have sandwiches. Think about it: no peanut butter and jelly sandwiches, bacon-cheeseburgers, Chicago hot dogs, or eggs Benedict. In this chapter you will find recipes representing sandwiches created around the globe, from naan to ciabatta to English muffins. Most of the recipes include serving suggestions.

Sourdough Hamburger Buns

Using the bread machine to mix and proof your dough makes this recipe easy. If you don't have a bread machine, feel free to adapt the recipe for Sourdough Poppy Seed Hot Dog Buns (page 86). Instead of a hot dog bun shape, make them into a hamburger bun shape. ***Makes 8 buns***

FOR ACTIVATING THE STARTER

9½ ounces (1 cup) sourdough starter

4 ounces (½ cup) lukewarm (90°F to 100°F) pure filtered or bottled water

4 ounces (1 cup) whole-wheat flour

FOR THE BREAD DOUGH

2 ounces (¼ cup) warm (100°F to 125°F) milk

2½ ounces (5 tablespoons) butter, melted, divided

1 egg

19 ounces (2 cups) active sourdough starter

2 tablespoons sugar

10 ounces (2½ cups) unbleached bread flour, plus more as needed

1 ounce (¼ cup) whole-wheat flour

1 teaspoon active dry yeast, or bread machine yeast

Nonstick cooking spray, for preparing the baking sheet

PRE-PREP TIME: 6 TO 12 HOURS TO ACTIVATE THE STARTER

SUGGESTED STARTER: WHOLE WHEAT

SOURDOUGH METHOD: AMBIENT

PREP TIME: 1 HOUR 40 MINUTES

BAKING TIME: 20 MINUTES

TOTAL TIME: 2 HOURS

 **Tools needed**
bread machine, pastry brush, baking sheet

To activate the starter

At least 6 to 12 hours before making the dough, in a medium bowl, combine the starter, lukewarm water, and flour, completely incorporating the ingredients into the starter. Loosely cover and let sit on the counter until ready to use.

To make the bread dough

1. In the bread pan of a bread machine, combine the milk, 3 tablespoons of butter, the egg, active starter, sugar, bread flour, and whole-wheat flour.

2. Using your finger, make a well in the top of the flours. Add the yeast to the well.

3. Place the bread pan into the bread machine. Set the machine on the dough cycle.

4. About 10 minutes after the dough cycle has started, check the dough. If it seems too dry, add 1 or 2 tablespoons of water. If it seems too wet, add 1 or 2 tablespoons of flour.

5. Lightly flour a breadboard or clean work surface, remove the dough from the machine, and place it on the prepared surface. Roll the dough into a log. Divide the log into 8 pieces.

6. Lightly coat a baking sheet with cooking spray.

7. Shape the dough pieces into balls and place them on the prepared baking sheet. Using a flat surface such as a plate, flatten the dough balls so they are about ¾ inch tall. Using a pastry brush, paint them with the remaining 2 tablespoons of melted butter.

8. Cover the hamburger buns with plastic wrap and let rise for 1 hour.

9. Preheat the oven to 350°F.

10. Remove the plastic wrap for the buns and bake them for 15 to 20 minutes, or until golden brown.

11. Let the buns cool slightly before slicing and serving.

Tip: Love cheeseburgers? Instead of melting the cheese on the burger, do it on the bun. Line a baking pan with aluminum foil. Lightly butter the inside of one half of a hamburger bun and place a slice of cheese on the other half. Place the halves, cut sides up, in the prepared pan. Preheat the broiler with an oven rack on the highest level. Place the pan into the oven but don't close the oven door. Broil until the cheese melts, paying careful attention while it's cooking. It can burn easily.

Sourdough Poppy Seed Hot Dog Buns

These homemade hot dog buns are so much tastier than those you can buy at the store. The poppy seeds were chosen to make buns for a Chicago dog. While the poppy seeds are optional, still paint the buns with the egg white to give the crust a shine. ***Makes 8 hot dog buns***

FOR ACTIVATING THE STARTER

9½ ounces (1 cup) sourdough starter

4 ounces (½ cup) lukewarm (90°F to 100°F) pure filtered or bottled water

4 ounces (1 cup) whole-wheat flour or (scant 1 cup) unbleached all-purpose flour

FOR THE BREAD DOUGH

12¾ ounces (3 cups) unbleached all-purpose flour, plus more for dusting

2 tablespoons sugar

1 teaspoon fine sea salt

19 ounces (2 cups) active sourdough starter

3 tablespoons butter, melted and cooled

4 ounces (½ cup) lukewarm (90°F to 100°F) milk

3 eggs, divided

Olive oil or nonstick cooking spray, for preparing the bowl and baking pan

Poppy seeds, for garnishing (optional)

PRE-PREP TIME: 6 TO 12 HOURS TO ACTIVATE THE STARTER

SUGGESTED STARTER: WHOLE WHEAT OR UNBLEACHED ALL-PURPOSE

SOURDOUGH METHOD: RETARDED

PREP TIME: 25 MINUTES, PLUS OVERNIGHT IN THE REFRIGERATOR

BAKING TIME: 20 MINUTES

TOTAL TIME: 45 MINUTES, PLUS OVERNIGHT IN THE REFRIGERATOR

Tools needed

stand mixer, 9-by-13-inch baking pan, pastry brush

To activate the starter

At least 6 to 12 hours before making the dough, in a medium bowl, combine the starter, lukewarm water, and flour, completely incorporating the ingredients into the starter. Loosely cover and let sit on the counter until ready to use.

To make the bread dough

1. In a medium bowl, stir together the flour, sugar, and salt. Set aside.

2. In the bowl of a stand mixer fitted with the dough hook, or in a large bowl, stir together the active starter, butter, milk, and two eggs.

3. With the mixer on low speed, or stirring with a wooden spoon, gradually add the dry ingredients to the wet ingredients, mixing until the ingredients are combined enough to be kneaded.

4. With the mixer on low speed, knead the dough until it's smooth and shiny, about 5 minutes. Alternately, lightly

flour a breadboard or clean work surface and turn the dough out on to it. Knead for 10 minutes by hand.

5. Coat a large bowl with olive oil and transfer the dough to it, turning to coat all sides. Cover the dough with plastic wrap and refrigerate overnight.

6. The next day, uncover the bowl and let the dough come to room temperature (75°F) before moving on to the next steps.

7. Once the dough is at room temperature, let it sit for 15 to 20 minutes more.

8. Flour a breadboard or clean work surface and turn the dough out on to it. Roll the dough into a log. Divide the log into 8 pieces. Working with one piece at a time, shape it into a rectangle. Fold the rectangle into thirds by folding in each end and pressing the seams together. Using both hands, roll the piece into a snake shape about 5 inches long. Even up the ends.

9. Preheat the oven to 400°F.

10. Lightly coat a 9-by-13-inch baking pan with cooking spray and transfer the hot dog buns to it.

11. Separate the remaining egg, and discard or save the yolk. In a small bowl, lightly beat the egg white with 2 teaspoons of water. Using a pastry brush, brush the egg white over the top of each bun.

12. Generously sprinkle each bun with poppy seeds (if using).

13. Bake the buns for 14 to 17 minutes until lightly brown.

14. Transfer the buns to a wire rack to cool completely.

Classic White Sourdough Bread Machine Bread

These days anyone can make homemade bread, especially if you have a bread machine. Not that it can't be done, but it is unusual to find sourdough recipes specifically for a bread machine. This loaf tastes quite good. The only difference in making a sourdough bread in the bread machine is the holes—you won't find as many of them. ***Makes 1 loaf***

FOR ACTIVATING THE STARTER

4¾ ounces (½ cup) sourdough starter

4 ounces (½ cup) lukewarm (90°F to 100°F) pure filtered or bottled water

4 ounces (scant 1 cup) unbleached bread flour

FOR THE BREAD DOUGH

2½ ounces (⅓ cup) room temperature (75°F) pure filtered or bottled water, plus more as needed

7 ounces (¾ cup) active sourdough starter

1 tablespoon plus 2 teaspoons butter, at room temperature

1 tablespoon plus 2 teaspoons sugar

¾ teaspoon fine sea salt

12¾ ounces (3 cups) unbleached all-purpose flour, or unbleached bread flour, plus more as needed

1½ teaspoons bread machine yeast, or instant yeast

PRE-PREP TIME: 6 TO 12 HOURS TO ACTIVATE THE STARTER

SUGGESTED STARTER: UNBLEACHED BREAD FLOUR

SOURDOUGH METHOD: AMBIENT

PREP TIME: 15 MINUTES

BAKING TIME: 3 HOURS

TOTAL TIME: 3 HOURS, 15 MINUTES

 *Tools needed*

bread machine

To activate the starter

At least 6 to 12 hours before putting the ingredients in the bread machine, in a medium bowl, combine the starter, lukewarm water, and flour, completely incorporating the ingredients into the starter. Loosely cover and let sit on the counter until ready to use.

To make the bread dough

1. In the bread pan of a bread machine, combine the room temperature water, active starter, butter, sugar, salt, flour, and yeast. Close the machine and, depending on your machine, use the White or Basic bread cycle.

2. About 10 minutes after the dough cycle has started, check the dough: If it is too dry, add 1 tablespoon or so of water. Check again in a few minutes. If it's still too dry, add a bit more water. If the dough is too wet, add 1 tablespoon of flour. Repeat again in about 2 minutes. The entire process in the bread machine takes about 3 hours.

Tip: Imagine it's dinnertime. The table is set. The kitchen is completely clean and the meal hasn't been served yet. All you have sitting on one counter is a slow cooker filled with the world's best chili or stew. On another counter is a bread machine that just started beeping an alert signaling the bread is done. How wonderful would that be?

Sourdough English Muffins

When talking of nooks and crannies, thoughts instantly go to English muffins. They are called English muffins even though they are closer to a true English crumpet than an American muffin, such as a blueberry muffin. Crumpets are holey on the top, but not in the middle. Not all English muffins are made with a sourdough starter, but the most well-known ones are. ***Makes 16 muffins***

FOR ACTIVATING THE STARTER

4¾ ounces (½ cup) sourdough starter

4 ounces (½ cup) lukewarm (90°F to 100°F) pure filtered or bottled water

4 ounces (1 cup) whole-wheat flour or (scant 1 cup) unbleached all-purpose flour

FOR THE ENGLISH MUFFIN DOUGH

9½ ounces (1 cup) active sourdough starter

16 ounces (2 cups) milk

19 ounces (4½ cups) unbleached all-purpose flour, whole-wheat flour, unbleached bread flour, or a mixture, divided, plus more for dusting

2 tablespoons sugar

2 teaspoons baking soda

2 teaspoons fine sea salt

Cornmeal, for dusting

Olive oil or nonstick cooking spray, for your hands

Butter, for cooking

PRE-PREP TIME: 6 TO 12 HOURS TO ACTIVATE THE STARTER

SUGGESTED STARTER: WHOLE WHEAT OR UNBLEACHED ALL-PURPOSE

SOURDOUGH METHOD: RETARDED

PREP TIME: 2 HOURS 12 MINUTES, PLUS OVERNIGHT REST

BAKING TIME: 10 MINUTES PER BATCH

TOTAL TIME: 2 HOURS 22 MINUTES, PLUS OVERNIGHT REST

Tools needed

cast iron skillet, or electric or stovetop flattop griddle

To activate the starter

At least 6 to 12 hours before making the dough, in a medium bowl, combine the starter, lukewarm water, and flour, completely incorporating the ingredients into the starter. Loosely cover and let sit on the counter until ready to use.

To make the English muffin dough

1. The day before serving, in a large bowl, stir together the active starter, milk, and 4 cups of all-purpose flour until combined. Cover the bowl with plastic wrap and let rest overnight (8 to 12 hours). If it will be longer, refrigerate the dough.

2. Early in the morning, if the dough is cold, let it sit out for about 1 to 2 hours to come to room temperature (75°F).

3. Lightly flour a breadboard or clean work surface.

4. Add the remaining ½ cup of flour, the sugar, baking soda, and salt to the dough. Knead them, in the bowl, into the dough, for at least 2 minutes.

5. Sprinkle enough cornmeal into a large baking pan, or on a large piece of parchment paper, to almost cover the surface.

6. There are two ways to form the English muffins:

   o Using a ½-cup measuring cup or an ice cream scoop, scoop out similar-size pieces of dough. Coat your hands with olive oil and pick up a piece of dough. Shape the dough into a hamburger patty shape, about ½ inch thick.

   o Or, using a lightly floured rolling pin, roll out the dough to ½-inch thickness. Using a 3-inch round cookie cutter, cut out the muffins. Grab the scraps and roll them into a ball. Let rest for a few minutes before repeating the process.

7. As the muffins are formed, place them into the prepared pan, turning to coat both sides with cornmeal. Once all the muffins are in the pan, let them rest while heating the skillet, or grill, over medium-low heat.

8. Once the skillet is hot, melt 1 teaspoon of butter in it just before adding each muffin to the pan. Cook the muffins for 3 to 5 minutes. Add more butter to the pan as you turn the muffins. Check to make sure they are not burning. Cook the second side for 3 minutes. The sides of the muffins should start to stiffen. Turn the muffins one more time. Cook for 2 minutes more.

9. Transfer the cooked muffins to a wire rack to cool. Cook the remaining muffins.

➤

10. Let the cooked muffins rest for a few minutes before splitting them. A bread knife is one choice for splitting the muffins. The more traditional way to split them is with a fork. Poke a fork into the outside edge of the muffin and repeat, making holes all the way around. Hold the muffin by the edges and gently pull the halves apart.

11. Split any leftover muffins and then place them on a baking sheet in the freezer overnight. The next day, transfer the frozen muffins into a resealable freezer bag, remove all the air, and seal. They will keep, frozen, for at least three months.

Tip: Sourdough English Muffins are good any time of day. Serve them slathered with peanut butter in the morning. Sliced turkey with mustard and watercress on an English muffin makes the perfect lunch sandwich. Sourdough English Muffins also make ideal hamburger buns.

Country Sourdough Sandwich Bread

Enjoy this simple recipe for sourdough sandwich bread. There aren't as many steps in this recipe, which means it's quicker to make. ***Makes 1 loaf***

FOR ACTIVATING THE STARTER

4¾ ounces (½ cup) sourdough starter

4 ounces (½ cup) lukewarm (90°F to 100°F) pure filtered or bottled water

4 ounces (1 cup) whole-wheat flour

FOR THE BREAD DOUGH

9½ ounces (1 cup) active sourdough starter

12¾ ounces (3 cups) whole berry, whole-wheat flour

4 ounces (½ cup) room temperature (75°F) pure filtered or bottled water

1½ teaspoons fine sea salt

PRE-PREP TIME: 6 TO 12 HOURS TO ACTIVATE THE STARTER

SUGGESTED STARTER: WHOLE WHEAT

SOURDOUGH METHOD: AMBIENT

PREP TIME: 12 HOURS 10 MINUTES

BAKING TIME: 1 HOUR

TOTAL TIME: 13 HOURS 10 MINUTES

Tools needed

9-by-5-inch bread pan

To activate the starter

At least 6 to 12 hours before making the dough, in a medium bowl, combine the starter, lukewarm water, and flour, completely incorporating the ingredients into the starter. Loosely cover and let sit on the counter until ready to use.

To make the bread dough

1. In a large bowl, stir together the active starter, whole-wheat flour, and room temperature water. Once it becomes too difficult to stir, knead in the ingredients with your hands. Let the dough rest for 10 minutes.

2. Add the salt and, in the bowl, knead it into the dough. The dough won't be overly stiff.

3. Place the dough into a 9-by-5-inch bread pan. Cover the pan with a clean kitchen towel and let sit in a warm place for 6 to 12 hours. The dough should double in size and have a domed top.

➤

4. Place the loaf in a cold oven. Turn the oven to 350°F.

5. Bake for 50 minutes to 1 hour until the top is golden brown and the loaf sounds hollow when thumped, or it reaches between 200°F and 210°F on a digital food thermometer.

6. Transfer to a wire rack to cool completely before slicing.

Tip: Getting even slices when cutting bread for sandwiches is important. The best way to do so is using an electric knife, especially when cutting through crusty bread. Electric knives are not very expensive. A decent one can be bought for less than $20. During Black Friday sales, they are often on sale for $10. Even better, check local thrift stores or yard sales where you may find one for only a couple of dollars.

Cinnamon-Raisin Sourdough Bread

This Cinnamon-Raisin Sourdough Bread is made very similarly to a cinnamon roll. The bread dough is rolled up around tons of cinnamon and brown sugar along with plenty of plump raisins, which are soaked in orange juice for a little flavor spike. You get to choose whether you prefer golden or black raisins. Dried cranberries make a good flavor variation as well. ***Makes 1 loaf***

FOR ACTIVATING THE STARTER
2 tablespoons sourdough starter

4 ounces (½ cup) lukewarm (90°F to 100°F) pure filtered or bottled water

4 ounces (1 cup) whole-wheat flour

FOR THE BREAD DOUGH
9½ ounces (1 cup) active sourdough starter

¾ cup warm (100°F to 125°F) pure filtered or bottled water

10 ounces (2½ cups) unbleached bread flour

4 ounces (1 cup) whole-wheat flour

1 teaspoon fine sea salt

3 tablespoons packed brown sugar

2 tablespoons melted butter

FOR THE FILLING
4 ounces (¾ cup) golden raisins, black raisins, or a mix

3 ounces (¼ cup plus 2 tablespoons) freshly squeezed orange juice, or water

3 tablespoons ground cinnamon

3 tablespoons packed light brown sugar

2 ounces (¼ cup) butter, melted and cooled

FOR THE BREAD PAN
1 tablespoon butter, melted and cooled

PRE-PREP TIME: 6 TO 12 HOURS TO ACTIVATE THE STARTER

SUGGESTED STARTER: WHOLE WHEAT

PREP TIME: 4 HOURS, PLUS OVERNIGHT DOUGH RISE

BAKING TIME: 30 MINUTES

TOTAL TIME: 4 HOURS 30 MINUTES, PLUS OVERNIGHT DOUGH RISE

Tools needed
stand mixer, 9-by-5-inch bread pan

To activate the starter
At least 6 to 12 hours before making the dough, in a medium bowl, combine the starter, lukewarm water, and flour, completely incorporating the ingredients into the starter. Loosely cover and let sit on the counter until ready to use.

To start the bread dough
1. The evening before baking the bread, in the bowl of a stand mixer fitted with the dough hook, or a large bowl, stir together the active starter and warm water. Add the bread flour, whole-wheat flour, salt, brown sugar, and butter. Mix on low speed, or stir with a wooden spoon, until all the ingredients are fully incorporated.

2. Knead the dough, in the bowl, on low speed, or by hand, until it stops sticking to the bowl. This step is much easier if you use a stand mixer. Cover the bowl with a clean kitchen towel and let rise overnight.

➤

To make the filling

1. The next morning, in a tall container or bowl, combine the raisins and orange juice and swish them around a bit. Set the raisins aside to absorb the juice.

2. In a small bowl, stir together the cinnamon and brown sugar and set aside.

To finish the bread dough

1. Lightly flour a breadboard or clean work surface and turn the dough out on to it. Using lightly floured hands, push the dough into a rectangular shape no wider than your bread pan and about ½ inch thick. If necessary, use a lightly floured rolling pin to get the dough into shape.

2. With a pastry brush, paint the dough with the ¼ cup of melted butter, leaving a 2-inch border all around the edges.

3. Evenly sprinkle the cinnamon and sugar mixture over the buttered dough.

4. Sprinkle the raisins on top of the cinnamon mixture.

5. Starting at the short end, roll up the dough. Don't roll it too tightly, but enough to keep the raisins inside. Fold the ends up over the seam of the bread dough.

6. Pour the 1 tablespoon of melted and cooled butter into a 9-by-5-inch bread pan. Tilt it back and forth to cover the bottom of the pan evenly. Carefully pick up the bread dough and place it into the pan, seam-side up, letting the butter coat the dough. Pick up the dough once, turn it over, and place it back in the pan, seam-side down.

7. Cover the pan with a clean kitchen towel and let rise in a warm, draft-free place for at least 4 hours.

8. Preheat the oven to 400°F.

9. Bake the bread for 30 minutes until the crust is golden brown and puffed up over the top of the pan.

10. Transfer the bread to a wire rack to cool completely.

Tip: The best way to enjoy Cinnamon-Raisin Sourdough Bread is to make French toast in an egg batter. If possible, allow slices of the bread to dry out a little before using them. In a shallow bowl large enough to hold one slice of bread, whisk 1 egg, 2 ounces (¼ cup) of milk, 1 teaspoon of ground cinnamon, and 1 teaspoon of vanilla extract. In a skillet over medium-high heat, melt a little butter. Dip one bread slice into the egg mixture and turn to coat both sides before placing the bread in the skillet. Repeat with another slice if there is room in the pan. Repeat to cook two more slices of bread after the first two have cooked.

Pullman Bread

Just hearing the name "Pullman bread" conjures up images of people having exotic adventures while traveling by train. The bread got its name from the pan named after Pullman train cars. The pans are 4 inches deep and 4 inches wide, and they can be anywhere from 13 to 16 inches long. All have a sliding lid, which helps prevent the normal domed top found on most breads. It is easier to stack bread with flat tops thus taking up less room in a small train kitchen. The bread itself is similar to the regular bread loaves you find in the grocery store. Typically, they are a white bread with completely square slices. ***Makes 1 loaf***

FOR ACTIVATING THE STARTER

9½ ounces (1 cup) sourdough starter

4 ounces (½ cup) lukewarm (90°F to 100°F) pure filtered or bottled water

4 ounces (1 cup) whole-wheat flour, (scant 1 cup) unbleached all-purpose flour, or (heaping 1 cup) rye flour

FOR THE BREAD DOUGH

19 ounces (2 cups) active sourdough starter

4 ounces (½ cup) lukewarm (90°F to 100°F) pure filtered or bottled water

10½ ounces (2½ cups) unbleached all-purpose flour, plus more for dusting

1½ teaspoons instant yeast

1½ teaspoons fine sea salt

1½ teaspoons sugar

Olive oil or nonstick cooking spray, for preparing the bowl

Butter, for preparing the Pullman bread pan

PRE-PREP TIME: 6 TO 12 HOURS TO ACTIVATE THE STARTER

SUGGESTED STARTER: WHOLE WHEAT, WHITE, RYE

SOURDOUGH METHOD: AMBIENT

PREP TIME: 1 HOUR 45 MINUTES

BAKING TIME: 45 MINUTES

TOTAL TIME: 2 HOURS 30 MINUTES

Tools needed

stand mixer, Pullman loaf pan

To activate the starter

At least 6 to 12 hours before making the dough, in a medium bowl, combine the starter, lukewarm water, and flour, completely incorporating the ingredients into the starter. Loosely cover and let sit on the counter until ready to use.

To make the bread dough

1. In the bowl of a stand mixer fitted with a dough hook, or a large bowl, combine the active starter, lukewarm water, flour, yeast, salt, and sugar. Mix on low speed for 7 to 10 minutes in the stand mixer, or 15 to 20 minutes stirring by hand.

2. Coat a large bowl with olive oil and transfer the dough to it, turning to coat all sides. Cover the bowl with a clean kitchen towel and let rise for about 1 hour.

3. Generously coat the bottom of the Pullman bread pan and the inside of the lid with butter.

4. Flour a breadboard or clean work surface and turn the dough out on to it. Shape the dough into a rectangle with a width no longer than the Pullman bread pan. Fold the bread dough from the right side to just past the middle of the dough. Fold the dough from the left side over the side just folded. Now roll the dough away from you to the top. Place the rolled dough, seam-side down, into the prepared pan. Cover the pan with its lid and let the dough rise in the pan for 20 to 25 minutes.

5. Preheat the oven to 350°F.

6. Bake the loaf for 40 to 45 minutes. During the last 5 minutes of baking, remove the lid. This will help form a crust.

7. Remove the loaf from the pan and transfer to a wire rack to cool completely.

Tip: The French call this bread *pain de mie*. *Pain* means "bread" and *de mie* means "soft," as in the soft part of the bread in the crumb (inside) area. In France, this bread is typically only sold in stores. Its shape is just like our sandwich bread. To get those even slices, use a good quality bread knife or an electric knife.

Sourdough Naan

Naan is an Indian bread made with yeast. Traditionally it's baked in a tandoori oven but can also be cooked on a flattop griddle or in a heavy pan such as a cast iron skillet. There are several recipes for naan out there. Some use yogurt, honey, and eggs. This one is made with yogurt and butter.
Makes 8 pieces

FOR ACTIVATING THE STARTER

4¾ ounces (½ cup) sourdough starter

4 ounces (½ cup) lukewarm (90°F to 100°F) pure filtered or bottled water

4 ounces (1 cup) whole-wheat flour or (scant 1 cup) unbleached all-purpose flour

FOR THE BREAD DOUGH

4 ounces (1 cup) whole-wheat flour

4¼ ounces (1 cup) unbleached all-purpose flour

1 teaspoon baking powder

½ teaspoon fine sea salt

9½ ounces (1 cup) active sourdough starter

4 ounces (½ cup) warm (100°F to 125°F) milk

4⅓ ounces (¼ cup) nonfat Greek yogurt

2 ounces (½ stick) butter, melted and cooled, divided

Olive oil, for coating the dough

PRE-PREP TIME: 6 TO 12 HOURS TO ACTIVATE THE STARTER
SUGGESTED STARTER: WHOLE WHEAT OR WHITE
SOURDOUGH METHOD: AMBIENT
PREP TIME: 4 HOURS 30 MINUTES
BAKING TIME: 8 MINUTES
TOTAL TIME: 4 HOURS 38 MINUTES

Tools needed

stand mixer, flattop griddle or cast iron skillet, pastry brush

To activate the starter

At least 6 to 12 hours before making the dough, in a medium bowl, combine the starter, lukewarm water, and flour, completely incorporating the ingredients into the starter. Loosely cover and let sit on the counter until ready to use.

To make the bread dough

1. In the bowl of a stand mixer fitted with a dough hook, or a large bowl, stir together the whole-wheat flour, all-purpose flour, baking powder, and salt.

2. In a small bowl, whisk the active starter, milk, yogurt, and 1 tablespoon of melted butter. Add the wet ingredients to the dry ingredients and mix on low speed, or stir by hand, to combine. The mixture will be stiff. Knead the dough on low speed for at least 5 minutes, or 10 minutes by hand. Lightly coat the outside of the entire dough ball with a bit of olive oil. Cover the bowl with a clean damp kitchen towel and let rise for 4 hours.

3. Lightly flour a breadboard or clean work surface and turn the dough out on to it. Divide the dough into 8 pieces. Cover the dough with a clean kitchen towel and let rest for 30 minutes.

4. Preheat your griddle or cast iron skillet over medium-high heat.

5. Using a floured rolling pin, roll each dough ball into a thin, round piece, about ¼ inch thick.

6. Sprinkle a couple drops of water onto the cooking surface. When the water sizzles, it's time to cook the naan. Using a pastry brush, brush one side of the dough pieces with some of the remaining 3 tablespoons of melted butter and place 2 pieces at a time, buttered-side down, into the skillet. As soon as the edges bubble, about 1 minute, brush the top of the naan with melted butter. Turn to cook on the other side. The naan should be done in about 2 minutes. Repeat to cook all the naan.

7. Naan freezes beautifully. Place it in an airtight resealable freezer bag for freezing, where it will keep for up to three months.

Tip: Naan can be eaten just the way it is or topped with delicious goodies. Personal pizzas are always a favorite. To make naan pizza, spread each naan with pizza sauce. Sprinkle with shredded mozzarella cheese and add your favorite toppings, such as sliced pepperoni and bell pepper. Place a baking stone sprinkled with cornmeal or semolina in the oven. Preheat the oven to 400°F. Carefully place the pizzas on the heated baking stone and bake for 10 to 12 minutes, or until the cheese is melted and bubbly.

Ciabatta

Oddly enough, ciabatta hasn't been around that long. It was invented in Italy in the early 1980s by a baker who was losing business due to French baguettes being imported to make sandwiches. The soft inside and sturdy crust of ciabatta is ideal for making sandwiches. ***Makes 1 loaf***

FOR ACTIVATING THE STARTER

9½ ounces (1 cup) sourdough starter

4 ounces (½ cup) lukewarm (90°F to 100°F) pure filtered or bottled water

4 ounces (1 cup) whole-wheat flour

FOR THE BREAD DOUGH

12 ounces (1¼ cups) active sourdough starter

1 teaspoon instant dry yeast

6½ ounces (1½ cups) unbleached bread flour, plus more for dusting

1 tablespoon fine sea salt

1 teaspoon sugar

2 ounces (¼ cup) lukewarm (90°F to 100°F) milk

3 tablespoons olive oil, plus more for coating the bowl

Cornmeal or semolina flour, for dusting

PRE-PREP TIME: 6 TO 12 HOURS TO ACTIVATE THE STARTER

SUGGESTED STARTER: WHOLE WHEAT

SOURDOUGH METHOD: AMBIENT

PREP TIME: 4 HOURS 10 MINUTES

BAKING TIME: 20 MINUTES

TOTAL TIME: 4 HOURS 30 MINUTES

Tools needed

stand mixer or handheld electric mixer, baking sheet

To activate the starter

At least 6 to 12 hours before making the dough, in a medium bowl, combine the starter, lukewarm water, and flour, completely incorporating the ingredients into the starter. Loosely cover and let sit on the counter until ready to use.

To make the bread dough

1. The next day, in the bowl of a stand mixer fitted with the dough hook, or a large bowl, combine the active starter, yeast, flour, salt, sugar, milk, and olive oil. Mix on low for a few seconds, or stir by hand. Increase the speed to number two and mix for 6 minutes until all the ingredients are well incorporated, or stir by hand.

2. Generously coat a large bowl with olive oil and transfer the dough to it, turning to coat all sides. Cover the bowl with a clean kitchen towel and place the bowl in the oven, with the light on, to rise for 1 to 2 hours, or until the dough doubles in size.

3. Flour a breadboard or clean work surface and turn the dough out on to it. Stretch the dough out. Fold it into thirds, folding from one end and then from the other. Stretch the dough into a rectangle. Re-cover the dough and let rise for 1 hour.

4. Sprinkle a baking sheet with cornmeal and place the ciabatta loaf on it. Dock the dough using your middle knuckle or fingertips to punch indentations evenly over the dough. This will keep the dough from bubbling up. Re-cover the dough and let rise 1 hour more in a warm, draft-free place.

5. Preheat the oven to 500°F.

6. Bake the ciabatta for 10 minutes. Reduce the oven temperature to 450°F and bake for 8 to 10 minutes more until lightly browned.

7. Transfer the baking sheet to a wire rack and let sit for 10 minutes. Transfer the ciabatta to the wire rack to cool completely.

Tip: The most famous sandwich made with a ciabatta is a bruschetta. One of my favorites is made on a lightly toasted piece of ciabatta topped with chopped fresh tomatoes, garlic, and basil leaves. In a small bowl, stir together 6 or 7 peeled, chopped plum tomatoes; 2 garlic cloves, minced; and 6 coarsely chopped fresh basil leaves. Stir in 1 tablespoon of olive oil, 1 teaspoon of balsamic vinegar, and season with salt and pepper. Set aside.

Preheat the broiler and line a baking sheet with aluminum foil. Slice the ciabatta, at an angle, into even slices. Paint one side of the slices with olive oil. Place the slices, oiled-side down, on the prepared baking sheet. Toast the bread under the broiler for a few minutes, watching carefully so it doesn't burn.

To serve the bruschetta, invert the slices onto a serving platter and top with the tomato mixture.

Sourdough Pita Bread

Pita is a Middle Eastern bread that has been around for about 4,000 years. It makes a nice alternative to regular sandwich bread, as just about any regular sandwich filling can be put into a pita pocket. When it's quartered, pita is often used like a dinner roll with a meal or as part of an appetizer. ***Makes 8 pitas***

FOR ACTIVATING THE STARTER

4¾ ounces (½ cup) sourdough starter

4 ounces (½ cup) lukewarm (90°F to 100°F) pure filtered or bottled water

4 ounces (1 cup) whole-wheat flour

FOR THE BREAD DOUGH

4¾ ounces (½ cup) active sourdough starter

10½ ounces (1⅓ cups) room temperature (75°) pure filtered or bottled water

2 tablespoons olive oil, or melted and cooled butter, plus more for preparing the bowl

5 ounces (1¼ cups) whole-wheat flour, plus more for dusting

1½ teaspoons fine sea salt

PRE-PREP TIME: 6 TO 12 HOURS TO ACTIVATE THE STARTER

SUGGESTED STARTER: WHOLE WHEAT, OR OTHER OF CHOICE

SOURDOUGH METHOD: AMBIENT

PREP TIME: 1 HOUR 30 MINUTES

BAKING TIME: 3 MINUTES PER BATCH

TOTAL TIME: 1 HOUR 33 MINUTES

Tools needed

baking stone, flattop griddle, or cast iron skillet

To activate the starter

At least 6 to 12 hours before making the dough, in a medium bowl, combine the starter, lukewarm water, and flour, completely incorporating the ingredients into the starter. Loosely cover and let sit on the counter until ready to use.

To make the bread dough

1. In a large bowl, stir together the active starter, room temperature water, and oil. Add the flour and salt, stirring until the flour is completely incorporated. When stirring becomes too difficult, knead them in, in the bowl. If the dough becomes too sticky, add more flour, 1 tablespoon at a time. Let the dough rest for 20 minutes.

2. Knead the dough for 10 minutes more until soft and elastic.

3. Coat another large bowl with olive oil and transfer the bread dough to it, turning to coat all sides.

4. Cover the bowl with a clean kitchen towel and let rise for 1 hour.

5. Lightly flour a breadboard or clean work surface and turn the dough out on to it. Shape the dough into a log and cut the log into 8 pieces.

6. Roll each piece into a ball, placing them on the floured surface. Slightly flatten each ball. Using a floured rolling pin, roll each into a 6- to 8-inch round, at least ⅛ inch thick.

7. Cover the pita doughs with a clean damp kitchen towel and let them rest while you preheat the oven.

8. Place a baking stone in the oven and preheat the oven to 475°F.

9. Place as many pitas as you can fit on the hot baking stone. Bake for 2 minutes, flip, and bake for 1 minute more. They should be puffed and lightly brown. Transfer to a wire rack to cool.

Alternately, the pitas can be cooked in a heavy-duty skillet or on a flattop griddle on the stovetop. Preheat the griddle or skillet over medium-high heat. Sprinkle a couple drops of water onto the cooking surface. When the water sizzles, it's time to cook the pitas. Place them on the griddle and cook until they puff up. Transfer to a wire rack to cool.

Tip: Pitas are often used as part of an appetizer. I like them served warm with a black olive tapenade. You'll wow them with your homemade Sourdough Pita Bread served with home-made tapenade. To make the tapenade: In a blender, combine 1¾ cups of pitted black olives, 1 garlic clove, peeled, and 3 tablespoons of olive oil. Press the blend button a couple of times. Open the lid and add a little salt and pepper. Hit the blend button a couple more times and you're done. Using a rubber spatula, transfer the tapenade into a small serving bowl. Place the bowl on a serving tray. Quarter the pitas and decoratively arrange the slices around the bowl. Serve with cocktail napkins.

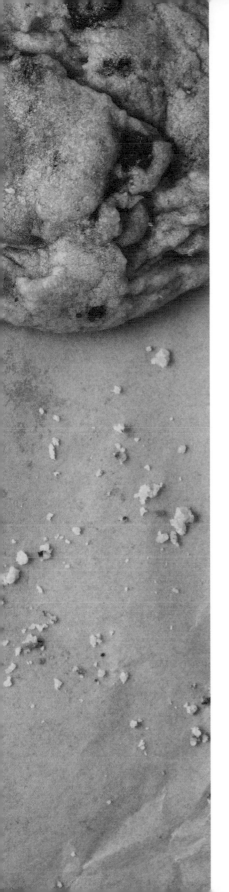

Chapter Six
SWEETS AND TREATS FOR LEFTOVER STARTER

During a consistent sourdough starter feeding schedule, you may have to remove some of your original starter to make room for the additional flour and water for feeding. Use the left-over sourdough starter in just about anything made with flour, including pizza dough, pretzels, waffles, cookies, and cake.

Coconut Sourdough Pancakes

Some people may find coconut overly sweet. Well, it's not sweet in this recipe due to the sourdough starter. If you're not a big coconut fan, skip it and substitute regular milk for the coconut milk. The coconut extract isn't necessary either; use vanilla instead. Add two tablespoons of sugar, if desired. ***Makes 10 pancakes***

FOR ACTIVATING THE STARTER

4¾ ounces (½ cup) sourdough starter

4 ounces (½ cup) lukewarm (90°F to 100°F) pure filtered or bottled water

4 ounces (1 cup) whole-wheat flour or buckwheat flour

FOR THE PANCAKE BATTER

4¼ ounces (1 cup) unbleached all-purpose flour

1 teaspoon baking soda

½ teaspoon fine sea salt

1 ounce (½ cup) flaked coconut

9½ ounces (1 cup) active sourdough starter

2 tablespoons butter, melted and cooled

1 egg

6 ounces (¾ cup) coconut milk

½ teaspoon coconut extract

PRE-PREP TIME: 6 TO 12 HOURS TO ACTIVATE THE STARTER

SUGGESTED STARTER: WHOLE WHEAT OR BUCKWHEAT FLOUR

SOURDOUGH METHOD: AMBIENT

PREP TIME: 15 MINUTES

BAKING TIME: 2 MINUTES PER BATCH

TOTAL TIME: 17 MINUTES

Tools needed

flattop griddle or cast iron skillet

To activate the starter

At least 6 to 12 hours before making the dough, in a medium bowl, combine the starter, lukewarm water, and flour, completely incorporating the ingredients into the starter. Loosely cover and let sit on the counter until ready to use.

To make the pancake batter

1. In a small bowl, stir together the flour, baking soda, salt, and coconut and set it aside.

2. In a large bowl, stir together the active starter, butter, egg, coconut milk, and coconut extract.

3. Add the dry ingredients to the wet ingredients and stir until just combined.

4. Preheat a cast iron skillet or a griddle over medium to medium-high heat. Sprinkle a couple drops of water onto the cooking surface. When the water sizzles, it's time to cook the pancakes. Pour in ½ cup of pancake batter for each pancake.

5. Cook until you see bubbles around the edges, then flip. Cook until the pancakes easily slide around the pan. You can lift one edge to peek and make sure they are not burning. Set the cooked pancakes on a plate and cover with paper towels to keep warm. If they do cool slightly, microwave them for about 10 seconds, or use a 250°F oven to keep them warm. Place an aluminum foil–covered baking sheet with an oven-safe dinner plate on it in the oven. Add the pancakes as needed and cover the plate with a clean kitchen towel.

6. Repeat with the remaining batter (it should make 10 pancakes, but if the coconut isn't used, there will be fewer). Serve these pancakes topped with a pat of butter and warm pure maple syrup.

Tip: Just mention coconut and the mind immediately goes to warmer climates and the tropics. Instead of using maple syrup, why not make your own syrup? Place orange or pineapple marmalade into a microwavable bowl or measuring cup. Heat it in the microwave until it melts and drizzle it over these coconut pancakes.

Pecan Waffles

Waffles aren't just for breakfast anymore. One of the favorite late-night treats at the 24-hour breakfast places is a pecan waffle topped with strawberries and whipped cream. It is the perfect coffee and dessert after a big night out. Of course, when making this at home, adding a scoop of vanilla ice cream won't hurt anything either. ***Makes 4 to 6 Belgian waffles***

FOR ACTIVATING THE STARTER

4¾ ounces (½ cup) sourdough starter

4 ounces (½ cup) lukewarm (90°F to 100°F) pure filtered or bottled water

4 ounces (1 cup) whole-wheat, buckwheat, or (scant 1 cup) unbleached all-purpose flour

FOR THE WAFFLE BATTER

3⅓ ounces (¾ cup) chopped pecans (optional)

5⅓ ounces (1¼ cups) unbleached all-purpose flour, or whole-wheat flour, or a combination

1 tablespoon sugar

2 teaspoons baking powder

½ teaspoon baking soda

½ teaspoon fine sea salt

9½ ounces (1 cup) active sourdough starter

4 ounces (1 stick) butter, melted and slightly cooled, plus more for serving

4 ounces (½ cup) milk

2 eggs

Nonstick cooking spray, for preparing the waffle iron

Pure maple syrup, for serving

PRE-PREP TIME: 6 TO 12 HOURS TO ACTIVATE THE STARTER

SUGGESTED STARTER: WHOLE WHEAT, BUCKWHEAT, OR UNBLEACHED ALL-PURPOSE

SOURDOUGH METHOD: AMBIENT

PREP TIME: 10 MINUTES

BAKING TIME: 5 MINUTES

TOTAL TIME: 15 MINUTES

Tools needed

waffle iron

To activate the starter

At least 6 to 12 hours before making the dough, in a medium bowl, combine the starter, lukewarm water, and flour, completely incorporating the ingredients into the starter. Loosely cover and let sit on the counter until ready to use.

To make the waffle batter

1. Toast the pecans in the microwave on high power for 1 minute. Add 30 seconds if you can't smell them yet. Alternately, toast the pecans in a 350°F oven for 5 to 7 minutes. Let the pecans cool while you make the waffle batter.

2. In a small bowl, whisk the flour, sugar, baking powder, baking soda, and salt. Set aside.

3. In a large bowl, whisk the active starter, butter, milk, and eggs.

4. Add the dry ingredients to the wet ingredients. Using a wooden spoon, stir until just combined. There will be lumps.

5. Heat the waffle iron according to the manufacturer's directions. Spray it with cooking spray.

6. Ladle ⅓ cup of batter onto the iron. Sprinkle 2 tablespoons of toasted pecans on top of the batter (if using). Close the lid and cook until golden brown. A good indication the waffle is almost done is when it stops steaming.

7. Repeat with the remaining batter.

8. Serve with butter and syrup. Peanut butter or other nut butters make tasty additions, too, plus they add a little protein to the meal.

Not serving the waffles right away? Just before making the waffles, preheat the oven to 200°F. Place a baking sheet with a wire rack on top inside. Add the waffles to the rack once cooked to keep them warm and crispy.

Tip: Why not make your own fruited syrup to go on these waffles? It's easy. In a small saucepan over medium heat, heat 1 cup of maple syrup. Add ¼ cup of blueberries, sliced strawberries, or cut mango. Bring the syrup to a boil. Boil for 1 to 2 minutes, mashing a few berries or some fruit. Use the syrup as is or strain out the fruit. To make the plate look pretty, add extra berries or mango when serving the waffles. Be sure to keep the syrup warm until it's served.

Sourdough Chocolate Chip Cookies with Several Flavor Variations

The best part about the sourdough in this recipe is that it cuts the sweetness and adds another flavor dimension for the palate. ***Makes 36 cookies***

FOR ACTIVATING THE STARTER

4¾ ounces (½ cup) sourdough starter

4 ounces (½ cup) lukewarm (90°F to 100°F) pure filtered or bottled water

4 ounces (1 cup) whole-wheat flour or (scant 1 cup) unbleached all-purpose

FOR THE COOKIE DOUGH

8 ounces (1¾ cups) chopped pecans, lightly toasted and still warm (see Pecan Waffles, page 110)

2 teaspoons fine sea salt, divided

19 ounces (4½ cups) unbleached all-purpose flour

2 teaspoons baking soda

1 pound (4 sticks) butter, at room temperature

14 ounces (2 cups) tightly packed brown sugar

5¼ ounces (¾ cup) granulated sugar

2 teaspoons vanilla extract

4 large eggs

9½ ounces (1 cup) active sourdough starter

24 ounces (4 cups) semisweet chocolate chips

Nonstick cooking spray, for preparing the baking sheets

PRE-PREP TIME: 6 TO 12 HOURS TO ACTIVATE THE STARTER
SUGGESTED STARTER: WHOLE WHEAT OR UNBLEACHED ALL-PURPOSE
SOURDOUGH METHOD: AMBIENT
PREP TIME: 30 MINUTES
BAKING TIME: 12 MINUTES
TOTAL TIME: 42 MINUTES

 *Tools needed*

stand mixer or handheld electric mixer, baking sheets

To activate the starter

At least 6 to 12 hours before making the dough, in a medium bowl, combine the starter, lukewarm water, and flour, completely incorporating the ingredients into the starter. Loosely cover and let sit on the counter until ready to use.

To make the cookie dough

1. While the toasted pecans are still warm, sprinkle with 1 teaspoon of salt and mix it in. Set the pecans aside.

2. In a medium bowl, whisk the flour, baking soda, and remaining 1 teaspoon of salt. Set aside.

3. In the bowl of a stand mixer fitted with the flat paddle attachment, or a large bowl and using a handheld electric mixer, cream together the butter, brown sugar, and granulated sugar.

4. Add the vanilla, then one at a time, add the eggs, mixing until each is incorporated before adding the next.

5. Add the active starter and mix until fully incorporated.

6. With your mixer running on low speed (so the flour stays in the bowl!), gradually add ½ cup of the flour mixture. Continue adding ½-cup portions of the flour mixture until it is all incorporated into the dough.

7. By hand, stir in the chocolate chips and pecans.

8. Preheat the oven to 375°F. Lightly coat two large baking sheets with cooking spray or cover them with parchment paper. Silicone mats are good, too—whatever works.

9. Scoop ⅛-cup (a coffee scoop) or heaping-tablespoon portions of dough onto the prepared baking sheets. The cookies will spread as they cook so don't put them too close together.

10. Place one sheet on the upper rack and one on the lower rack. Bake for 10 to 12 minutes, rotating the baking sheets halfway through the baking time from one shelf to the other and turning them 180 degrees (front to back). Use your nose—if the cookies are done, you'll smell them.

11. Transfer the baking sheets to wire racks to cool for 3 minutes. Remove the cookies from the sheets and cool completely on the racks. If stored in a cookie jar with a loose lid, the cookies will stay crispy. If stored in an airtight container, they will become softer.

Tip: There are 5¾ cups total of chocolate chips and pecans in this recipe. Feel free to use other add-ins instead. Here are a few suggestions: coconut, raisins, dried cranberries, other dried fruits, candied fruit, chopped-up candy bars (freeze them first so they are easier to cut), white chocolate chips, milk chocolate chips, mint chocolate chips, dark chocolate chips, butterscotch chips, peanut butter chips, rice cereal, corn flakes, raw nuts, other lightly salted nuts, banana chips, other dehydrated fruits, pretzels, marshmallows, etc.

Sourdough Tropical Carrot Cake

This cake is above and beyond other carrot cakes with the addition of pineapple and coconut. The sourdough cuts some of the sweetness. ***Makes 1 (9-by-13-inch) cake***

FOR ACTIVATING THE STARTER

4¾ ounces (½ cup) sourdough starter
4 ounces (½ cup) lukewarm (90°F to 100°F) pure filtered or bottled water
4 ounces (1 cup) whole-wheat flour

FOR THE CAKE BATTER

Nonstick cooking spray, for preparing the baking pan
8½ ounces (2 cups) unbleached all-purpose flour, plus more for preparing the baking pan
14 ounces (2 cups) sugar
1 teaspoon fine sea salt
1 teaspoon baking soda
9½ ounces (1 cup) active sourdough starter
8 ounces (1 cup) vegetable oil
4 eggs
8 ounces (2 cups) grated carrots
1 (20-ounce) can crushed pineapple, drained

FOR THE ICING

3 ounces (6 tablespoons) cream cheese, at room temperature
2 ounces (¼ cup) butter, at room temperature
9 ounces (2 cups) powdered sugar
1 teaspoon vanilla extract
2.2 ounces (½ cup) chopped pecans, lightly toasted (see Pecan Waffles, page 110)
1 ounce (½ cup) flaked coconut

PRE-PREP TIME: 6 TO 12 HOURS TO ACTIVATE THE STARTER
SUGGESTED STARTER: WHOLE WHEAT
SOURDOUGH METHOD: AMBIENT
PREP TIME: 25 MINUTES
BAKING TIME: 55 MINUTES
TOTAL TIME: 1 HOUR 20 MINUTES

Tools needed
9-by-13-inch baking pan

To activate the starter

At least 6 to 12 hours before making the dough, in a medium bowl, combine the starter, lukewarm water, and flour, completely incorporating the ingredients into the starter. Loosely cover and let sit on the counter until ready to use.

To make the cake batter

1. Preheat the oven to 325°F. Coat a 9-by-13-inch baking pan with cooking spray and flour the pan, knocking out any excess flour.

2. In a medium bowl, whisk the flour, sugar, salt, and baking soda.

3. In a large bowl, stir together the active starter, vegetable oil, and eggs.

4. Slowly add the dry ingredients to the wet ingredients, stirring until just mixed. There will be some lumps.

5. Stir in the carrots and pineapple. Pour the cake batter into the prepared pan and bake for 55 minutes, or until a toothpick inserted into the center comes out clean.

6. Transfer the pan to a wire rack and let the cake cool completely.

To make the icing

1. Once the cake is completely cool, make the icing: In a large bowl, using an electric handheld mixer, cream together the cream cheese and butter.

2. A little at a time, add the powdered sugar, mixing until all is incorporated.

3. Add the vanilla and mix it in.

4. By hand, stir in the toasted pecans and coconut.

5. Frost the cake with the cream cheese icing. Keep the cake refrigerated until serving and refrigerate any leftovers.

Tip: This cake freezes beautifully. Place the frosted cake on an aluminum foil–lined baking sheet and place it in the freezer overnight. The next day, remove the cake from the baking sheet and wrap it completely in plastic wrap and then place it in a resealable plastic bag. Place the bag in the freezer. It will keep for three months. Totally unwrap the cake before defrosting it. Place the cake in a cake container in the refrigerator to defrost.

Flavorful Focaccia Bread

Focaccia has been around since ancient Roman times. The top is always covered in olive oil, extra virgin being the best. A plain version may only have salt sprinkled on top of the oil. These days you'll easily find fancier versions with a plethora of other ingredients to choose from. Focaccia spread with cheese and fresh herbs is so satisfying it could be considered the major part of a meal. When considering some optional toppings, my favorites are fresh rosemary and Parmesan; red onion with salt and pepper; and sliced grape tomatoes with feta. The options are endless. ***Makes 12 pieces***

FOR ACTIVATING THE STARTER
4¾ ounces (½ cup) sourdough starter

4 ounces (½ cup) lukewarm (90°F to 100°F) pure filtered or bottled water

4 ounces (1 cup) whole-wheat flour

FOR THE FOCACCIA DOUGH
2¼ teaspoons active dry yeast

12 ounces (1½ cups) warm (100°F to 125°F) pure filtered or bottled water

9½ ounces (1 cup) active sourdough starter

2 teaspoons fine sea salt

1 tablespoon sugar

12¾ ounces (3 cups) unbleached all-purpose flour, divided

2 tablespoons butter, at room temperature

2 tablespoons olive oil, plus more for your hands and the plastic wrap

Freshly ground Himalayan salt, or other coarse salt

Freshly ground black pepper

PRE-PREP TIME: 6 TO 12 HOURS TO ACTIVATE THE STARTER
SUGGESTED STARTER: WHOLE WHEAT
SOURDOUGH METHOD: AMBIENT
PREP TIME: 1 HOUR 20 MINUTES
BAKING TIME: 30 MINUTES
TOTAL TIME: 1 HOUR 50 MINUTES

Tools needed
9-by-13-inch baking pan, or baking sheet

To activate the starter
At least 6 to 12 hours before making the dough, in a medium bowl, combine the starter, lukewarm water, and flour, completely incorporating the ingredients into the starter. Loosely cover and let sit on the counter until ready to use.

To make the focaccia dough
1. Early in the day, in a small bowl, sprinkle the yeast over the warm water. Let the yeast bloom for 10 minutes.

2. In a large bowl, stir together the active starter, bloomed yeast, sea salt, sugar, and 2 cups of flour. Once the mixture is well incorporated, add the remaining 1 cup of flour and, in the bowl, knead it in. Cover the bowl with a clean kitchen towel and let rise for 1 hour.

FOR THE TOPPINGS (ALL OPTIONAL DEPENDING ON TASTE)

Crushed or roasted garlic

Fresh or dried rosemary, oregano, basil, thyme, sage, marjoram, etc.

Grated or shredded Parmesan, Romano, or Pecorino cheese

Shredded sharp Cheddar, blue, feta, fresh mozzarella, or other cheese

Sliced jalapeño peppers

Thinly sliced baby portabella mushrooms

Thinly sliced plum, cherry, or grape tomatoes

Thinly sliced red onion

3. Punch down the dough and let it rest for 10 minutes.

4. Generously coat a 9-by-13-inch baking pan or baking sheet with the butter and transfer the dough to it.

5. With well-oiled hands, press the dough down to fill the pan or into a rectangle on the baking sheet until it is about 1 inch thick.

6. Using your middle knuckle, dock (make indentations in) the dough.

7. Drizzle the olive oil over the top of the dough, covering the entire surface.

8. Season the entire top with a few grinds of Himalayan salt and pepper, or choose some of the optional ingredients—alone or in combination.

9. Lightly coat a piece of plastic wrap with olive oil and cover the focaccia with it. Let rise for 30 minutes.

10. Preheat the oven to 425°F.

11. Bake the focaccia for 15 minutes. Reduce the oven temperature to 375°F and bake for 15 minutes more.

12. Transfer the focaccia to a wire rack to cool for 10 minutes before serving.

Tip: When using fresh as opposed to dried herbs in a recipe, you'll need twice as much fresh herb as dried. Speaking of herbs, if you ever want to grow your own, try rosemary first. It grows well in the ground or in a pot and will thrive in most climates. It likes full sun but it can also be grown indoors.

Sourdough Breadstick Twists

Everyone will enjoy these breadstick twists. They go great with soups and salads as well as a bowl of spaghetti and meatballs. They also make a tasty afternoon snack. Try dipping them in homemade pesto or marinara. Imagine eating one coated in a warm beer cheese dip. Yum.

Makes 8 twisted breadsticks

FOR ACTIVATING THE STARTER

9½ ounces (1 cup) sourdough starter

4 ounces (½ cup) lukewarm (90°F to 100°F) pure filtered or bottled water

4 ounces (1 cup) whole-wheat flour, (heaping 1 cup) rye flour, or (1 cup) pumpernickel

FOR THE BREAD DOUGH

6¾ ounces (scant 1¾ cups) whole-wheat flour, plus more for dusting

1 teaspoon sugar

1 teaspoon baking soda

1 teaspoon fine sea salt

9½ ounces (1 cup) active sourdough starter (refrigerate any remaining starter for future use)

Nonstick cooking spray, for preparing the baking sheet

1 egg white, beaten

Sesame seeds, for garnishing

PRE-PREP TIME: 6 TO 12 HOURS TO ACTIVATE THE STARTER

SUGGESTED STARTER: WHOLE WHEAT, RYE, OR PUMPERNICKEL

SOURDOUGH METHOD: AMBIENT

PREP TIME: 1 HOUR 20 MINUTES

BAKING TIME: 20 TO 25 MINUTES

TOTAL TIME: 1 HOUR 45 MINUTES

Tools needed
baking sheet

To activate the starter

At least 6 to 12 hours before making the dough, in a medium bowl, combine the starter, lukewarm water, and flour, completely incorporating the ingredients into the starter. Loosely cover and let sit on the counter until ready to use.

To make the bread dough

1. In a large bowl, stir together the flour, sugar, baking soda, and salt until completely combined.

2. Stir in the active starter. When the dough becomes too difficult to stir, knead the dough, in the bowl, by hand. Cover with a clean kitchen towel and let sit for 1 hour.

3. Lightly flour a breadboard or clean work surface and turn the dough out on to it. Roll the dough around and knead it a few times to remove some of the stickiness. Flatten the dough into a rectangular shape about 10 by 8 inches.

4. Using a floured knife, cut the dough into eight (1-inch-wide) sticks.

5. Lightly coat a baking sheet with cooking spray.

6. Stretch each dough stick to about 1 foot long. Fold them in half, twist, and seal the ends together. Place the twists on the prepared baking sheet.

7. Cover the baking sheet with a clean kitchen towel and place in a warm, draft-free place for 20 minutes.

8. Preheat the oven to 375°F.

9. Brush the bread sticks with the egg white and generously sprinkle with sesame seeds.

10. Bake the bread sticks for 20 to 25 minutes, or until they are golden brown and not too hard.

Tip: There are many flavorful options for garnishing these breadsticks. Try freshly ground Himalayan salt and pepper, grated Parmesan cheese, granulated garlic, red pepper flakes, poppy seeds, flaxseed, semolina, onion powder, sunflower seeds, chia seeds. What would you use?

Sourdough Pizza Dough

They say the average American eats about 46 slices of pizza a year. There is no reason you shouldn't make some of those slices yourself, especially if you start by making your own pizza crust. Putting sourdough starter in the dough adds another enjoyable flavor dimension to the pizza.
Makes 1 (12-inch) pizza crust

FOR ACTIVATING THE STARTER

14¼ ounces (1½ cups)
   sourdough starter
4 ounces (½ cup) warm (100°F to 125°F)
   pure filtered or bottled water
4 ounces (1 cup) whole-wheat flour

FOR THE PIZZA CRUST DOUGH

1 tablespoon olive oil
1 teaspoon freshly ground
   Himalayan salt
6½ ounces (1½ cups) unbleached bread
   flour, divided, plus more for dusting
Olive oil or nonstick cooking spray, for
   preparing the bowl
Cornmeal, for dusting
Pizza toppings, as desired, such as pizza
   sauce, grated or shredded cheese,
   pepperoni, sliced vegetables

PRE-PREP TIME: 6 TO 12 HOURS TO ACTIVATE THE STARTER
SUGGESTED STARTER: WHOLE WHEAT
SOURDOUGH METHOD: AMBIENT
PREP TIME: 2 HOURS
BAKING TIME: 15 MINUTES
TOTAL TIME: 2 HOURS 15 MINUTES

Tools needed
baking stone, baking sheet, pizza peel (optional)

To activate the starter

At least 6 to 12 hours before making the dough, in a medium bowl, combine the starter, lukewarm water, and flour, completely incorporating the ingredients into the starter. Loosely cover and let sit on the counter until ready to use.

To make the pizza crust dough

1. Two hours before making the pizza, in a large bowl, thoroughly mix together the entire amount of activated starter, olive oil, and salt. Add 1 cup of flour, stirring until it's completely incorporated.

2. Lightly flour a breadboard or a clean work surface and turn the dough out on to it. Begin kneading the dough, adding more flour if the dough is too wet. Knead for about 5 minutes. If the dough is still too wet, add a bit more flour. The dough should be soft and a little sticky. If it's really sticky, add more flour, 1 tablespoon at a time. If it's a bit too dry, add 1 tablespoon of water. Shape the dough into a ball.

3. Lightly coat a large bowl with olive oil and transfer the dough to it, turning to coat all sides. Cover the bowl with a plate or plastic wrap and let rest until it's time to make the pizza.

4. Sprinkle a baking stone with cornmeal and place the stone into the oven. Preheat the oven to 450°F.

5. On the floured surface, using a rolling pin, roll the dough into the size and thickness of your desired pizza. Dress the pizza however you would like.

6. If you don't have a pizza peel, sprinkle cornmeal on a rimless baking sheet or on an inverted sheet pan. Carefully slide the dressed pizza onto the prepared sheet. Very carefully, slide the pizza from the sheet onto the baking stone.

7. Bake the pizza for 10 to 15 minutes, depending on the toppings you've selected.

8. Using oven gloves and a heavy metal spatula, slide the pizza off the stone and back onto the baking sheet.

9. Slice and eat.

Tip: A special and popular pizza these days is a Margherita pizza. It is a fresh-tasting pizza made by lightly painting the pizza crust with pizza sauce, layering sliced plum tomatoes over the sauce, decoratively placing fresh sliced mozzarella on top, and finishing the whole thing with fresh basil leaves spread evenly among the tomato and cheese. The colors of the Italian flag—red, white, and green—are very prominent on this tasty pizza.

Double Piecrust

By adding your sourdough starter to this pie dough, it adds a bit of tanginess that counteracts the sweetness of the pie filling. If you are using this pie dough for a quiche, omit the sugar for an even stronger taste. ***Makes enough for 2 piecrusts***

FOR ACTIVATING THE STARTER
2.4 ounces (¼ cup) sourdough starter

4 ounces (½ cup) lukewarm (90°F to 100°F) pure filtered or bottled water

4 ounces (1 cup) whole-wheat flour

FOR THE PIECRUST DOUGH
9½ ounces (1 cup) active sourdough starter

8½ ounces (2 cups) unbleached all-purpose flour, or 8 ounces whole-wheat flour, plus more as needed

1 tablespoon sugar

½ teaspoon fine sea salt

12 ounces (3 sticks) cold butter

PRE-PREP TIME: 6 TO 12 HOURS TO ACTIVATE THE STARTER

SUGGESTED STARTER: WHOLE WHEAT

SOURDOUGH METHOD: RETARDED

PREP TIME: 8 HOURS

BAKING TIME: VARIES, DEPENDING ON THE BAKED PIE RECIPE

TOTAL TIME: 8 PLUS HOURS

Tools needed
food processor

To activate the starter
At least 6 to 12 hours before making the dough, in a medium bowl, combine the starter, lukewarm water, and flour, completely incorporating the ingredients into the starter. Loosely cover and let sit on the counter until ready to use.

To make the piecrust dough
1. After 6 hours, place 9½ ounces (1 cup) of the fed starter into the refrigerator. If keeping the leftover starter, place it in another container.

2. In a medium bowl, stir together the flour, sugar, and salt. Cover the bowl with plastic wrap and place it in the refrigerator.

3. Cut the butter into chunks and place them in a bowl or resealable plastic bag and then back into the refrigerator.

4. Early the next day, place the flour mixture in the food processor. Process a couple of times to make sure it's well mixed.

5. Add the cold butter pieces and process until they're well incorporated and the mixture looks like small peas.

6. Spoon in the active starter, starting with half, and process. Add half of the remaining starter and process. If the mixture has come together into a ball that is not too wet, too sticky, or too dry, the remaining starter may not be needed. If it is too wet, sticky, or dry, add a bit more starter. If that doesn't work, and it's too dry or sticky, add 1 tablespoon or so of water. If it's too wet, add 1 tablespoon of flour.

7. Remove the dough from the bowl of the food processor and form it into a ball. Place the ball in a large bowl. Cover the bowl with plastic wrap and let sit on the kitchen counter for at least 7 hours. If need be, it can sit for up to 12 hours.

8. Divide the dough into two equal halves—eyeball it or use a scale. They don't have to be exact.

9. Flatten the pieces into disks and wrap them in plastic wrap or parchment paper. Refrigerate for at least 1 hour.

10. Roll out the dough and cook according to the filled pie recipe you've chosen.

11. This pie dough will last up to one week if the wrapped disks are put into an airtight container or freezer bag and kept in the refrigerator. They also can be frozen for up to three months in freezer-safe wrapping.

Tip: One of the simplest pies to make is a chess pie, which is typically made with whatever is on hand—such as eggs, sugar, milk, and sometimes flour or cornmeal. Add a lemon—juice and zest—and you've got a lemon chess pie, which is really just the best part of a lemon meringue pie, the lemon filling without the meringue.

Southern Sourdough Biscuits

Biscuits, or at least something very similar, have been around for centuries, all over the world. More than any other culture, US Southerners strive to include these light, fluffy gems as a part of their daily meal. Buttermilk biscuits are the favorite. Buttermilk, though, isn't needed in this recipe, as the sourdough starter provides the sour taste here. Southern restaurants always have biscuits on their menus. Besides eating biscuits slathered in butter, they are often part of an all-in-one dish—biscuits and sausage gravy is very popular. An even more elaborate version, often called Eggs Benny, has each biscuit half layered with a sausage patty, a poached egg, and then smothered in sausage gravy. Who needs the English muffin version with ham and hollandaise sauce anyway? Besides eating biscuits with fried chicken, biscuits appear in dishes like chicken and dumplings. Yes, biscuits are used in desserts, too. Why make shortcake when you can serve your strawberries and whipped cream on a light and fluffy biscuit? ***Makes 8 biscuits***

FOR ACTIVATING THE STARTER
2.4 ounces (¼ cup) sourdough starter

4 ounces (½ cup) lukewarm (90°F to 100°F) pure filtered or bottled water

4 ounces (1 cup) whole-wheat flour

FOR THE BISCUIT DOUGH
2½ ounces (5 tablespoons) plus 1 teaspoon cold butter

4¼ ounces (1 cup) unbleached all-purpose, or 4 ounces whole-wheat flour, plus more for dusting

¾ teaspoon baking soda

¼ teaspoon fine sea salt

9½ ounces (1 cup) active sourdough starter

Nonstick cooking spray, for preparing the baking sheet

Melted butter, for brushing (optional)

PRE-PREP TIME: 6 TO 12 HOURS TO ACTIVATE THE STARTER

SUGGESTED STARTER: WHOLE WHEAT

SOURDOUGH METHOD: AMBIENT

PREP TIME: 15 MINUTES

BAKING TIME: 8 TO 10 MINUTES

TOTAL TIME: 25 MINUTES

 *Tools needed*
baking sheet, 2½-inch biscuit or cookie cutter, rolling pin

To activate the starter
At least 6 to 12 hours before making the dough, in a medium bowl, combine the starter, lukewarm water, and flour, completely incorporating the ingredients into the starter. Loosely cover and let sit on the counter until ready to use.

To make the biscuit dough
1. Cut the butter into small cubes and place them in a bowl or resealable plastic bag and then back into the refrigerator.

2. In a large bowl, stir together the flour, baking soda, and salt until completely combined.

3. With a pastry cutter or two knives in scissors fashion, cut the cold butter cubes into the flour mixture until the mixture resembles small peas.

4. Stir in the active starter.

5. Flour a breadboard or clean work surface and turn the biscuit dough out on to it. With lightly floured hands, gently knead the biscuit dough five times by folding the dough from one side to the other and from the top to the bottom. Do not overwork the dough or the biscuits will be tough.

6. With floured hands or a floured rolling pin, pat or roll the dough into a rectangular shape ½ inch thick. Cut the dough into 8 squares or use a 2½-inch biscuit or cookie cutter to cut out the biscuit rounds, dipping the knife or cutter into flour before each cut. Do not twist the cutter, as it will seal the edges and the biscuits will not rise in the oven.

7. Preheat the oven to 425°F. Lightly coat a baking sheet with cooking spray, or line it with parchment paper or a silicone baking mat.

8. Place the biscuits on the prepared baking sheet. Bake for 8 to 10 minutes until slightly risen and golden brown on top.

9. Using a pastry brush, paint each warm biscuit with melted butter (if using) as soon as they come out of the oven. Serve warm.

Tip: It is very important not to overwork biscuit dough. One way to ensure this is to make dropped biscuits. Big dropped biscuits are also known as cathead biscuits. To make dropped biscuits, just scoop up about one-sixth of the dough and drop it onto the prepared baking sheet and bake as directed. However, note that because they're larger, they will take longer to bake (10 to 12 minutes), so watch them.

Sourdough Pretzels

There is nothing tastier than homemade snacks. Got a small get-together coming up? Take these pretzels and watch people fight over who will get the last one. Plus, there won't be any mindless eating—they'll enjoy every bite. This recipe uses **unactivated** sourdough starter, so they'll be done even faster. ***Makes 12 pretzels***

12¾ ounces (3 cups) unbleached all-purpose flour, plus more for dusting

1 ounce (¼ cup) nonfat dry milk

1 tablespoon sugar

2 teaspoons instant yeast

1½ teaspoons fine sea salt

9½ ounces (1 cup) **unfed** sourdough starter

6 ounces (¾ cup) lukewarm (90°F to 100°F) pure filtered or bottled water

1 tablespoon butter, melted and slightly cooled

Nonstick cooking spray, for preparing the baking sheets

2 tablespoons baking soda

Freshly ground Himalayan salt

PRE-PREP TIME: NONE

SUGGESTED STARTER: WHOLE WHEAT

SOURDOUGH METHOD: AMBIENT

PREP TIME: 49 MINUTES

BAKING TIME: 12 MINUTES

TOTAL TIME: 1 HOUR 1 MINUTE

Tools needed

stand mixer or handheld electric mixer, medium pot, baking sheets

1. In a large bowl, whisk the flour, dry milk, sugar, yeast, and sea salt. Set aside.

2. In the bowl of a stand mixer fitted with the dough hook, or in a large bowl and using a handheld electric mixer, combine the unfed sourdough starter, lukewarm water, and butter. Turn the machine on low.

3. With the mixer running, slowly add the flour mixture. Continue to mix until the ingredients come together in a ball around the dough hook. If using a handheld mixer, mix as long as possible. When the dough becomes too stiff, use your hands or a rubber scraper to incorporate the rest of the flour into the dough. If the dough is too dry, add more water, 1 tablespoon at a time. If the dough is too wet, add flour, 1 tablespoon at a time.

4. Lightly sprinkle flour over the dough ball, cover with a clean kitchen towel, and set aside for 45 minutes in a warm, draft-free place.

5. Preheat the oven to 475°F. Coat two baking sheets with cooking spray.

6. Divide the dough into 12 pieces. The best way to do this is to weigh the dough and divide the weight by 12. Weigh each piece for the correct amount.

7. Roll each portion into a ball. Shape each ball into an 18-inch-long snake. Twist each piece into a pretzel shape, pressing the ends of the pretzels to make sure they stay in shape.

8. Place a wire rack on top of a clean kitchen towel.

9. Fill a medium pot halfway with water and bring to a boil over high heat. Stir in the baking soda.

10. Using tongs, place 2 or 3 pretzels (try not to overcrowd the pot) into the water and cook for 1 minute. Remove them from the water and place on the wire rack. Repeat with the remaining pretzels.

11. Place the boiled pretzels on the prepared baking sheets and sprinkle the pretzels with Himalayan salt.

12. Bake for 12 minutes and cool on wire racks before serving.

Tip: Want to make your own homemade mustard to go with your very own homemade pretzels? It's very simple. In a large bowl, stir together ½ cup of mustard powder, ½ cup of beer, 3 tablespoons of cider vinegar, 2 teaspoons of salt, and ⅓ cup of mustard seeds, crushed (in a resealable plastic bag, with your rolling pin, pushing down as you roll, or use a clean coffee grinder). Transfer to a quart-sized canning jar. Refrigerate for a day or two before eating. It will keep up to one year, refrigerated.

Sourdough Cinnamon-Sugar Doughnuts

The sourdough starter used in this doughnut recipe is a welcome addition. It helps cut the typical sweetness. The other good additions are the baking powder and baking soda. They add extra leavening, which shortens the normal rising time. ***Makes 12 doughnuts***

FOR ACTIVATING THE STARTER
2.4 ounces (¼ cup) sourdough starter
4 ounces (½ cup) lukewarm (90°F to 100°F) pure filtered or bottled water
4 ounces (1 cup) whole-wheat flour

FOR FRYING
2 quarts vegetable oil or peanut oil

FOR THE TOPPING
7 ounces (1 cup) sugar
2 teaspoons ground cinnamon

FOR THE DOUGHNUT DOUGH
9 ounces (2 cups) unbleached all-purpose flour, plus more for dusting
3½ ounces (½ cup) sugar
1 teaspoon baking powder
½ teaspoon baking soda
½ teaspoon fine sea salt
4¾ ounces (½ cup) active sourdough starter
1 egg
2½ ounces (⅓ cup) buttermilk
2 tablespoons vegetable oil
4 ounces (½ cup) butter, melted

PRE-PREP TIME: 6 TO 12 HOURS TO ACTIVATE THE STARTER
SUGGESTED STARTER: WHOLE WHEAT
SOURDOUGH METHOD: AMBIENT
PREP TIME: 30 MINUTES
BAKING TIME: 6 MINUTES
TOTAL TIME: 36 MINUTES

 *Tools needed*
heavy pot, rolling pin, doughnut cutter, candy/deep-fry thermometer

To activate the starter
At least 6 to 12 hours before making the dough, in a medium bowl, combine the starter, lukewarm water, and flour, completely incorporating the ingredients into the starter. Loosely cover and let sit on the counter until ready to use.

To prepare for frying the doughnuts
The morning of making the doughnuts, pour the vegetable oil into a large pot and place it on the stovetop. Don't heat it yet. Cover a wire rack with paper towels and set aside.

To make the topping
In a wide, shallow bowl, stir together the sugar and cinnamon until well mixed. Place it near the prepared wire rack.

To make the doughnut dough
1. In a medium bowl, whisk the flour, sugar, baking powder, baking soda, and salt until combined. Set aside.

2. In a large bowl, stir together the active starter, egg, buttermilk, and vegetable oil.

3. Slowly add the dry ingredients to the wet ingredients, stirring to combine.

4. Turn the heat under the oil to high and let the oil heat to 350°F.

5. Flour a breadboard or clean work surface and turn the dough out on to it. Knead the dough a few times to make sure all the ingredients stay together.

6. With a floured rolling pin, roll the dough ¾ inch thick.

7. Using a doughnut cutter dipped in flour so the dough doesn't stick, cut the dough. Re-roll the dough scraps to cut out the remaining doughnuts. Save the doughnut holes to cook, too.

8. Working with only 2 or 3 doughnuts at a time, carefully place them in the hot oil and fry for 2 to 3 minutes per side. They should be golden brown and fluffy. The doughnut holes will cook a little faster.

9. Using tongs, lift the doughnuts from the oil and quickly dip them into the cinnamon-sugar mixture.

10. Place them on the prepared wire rack to drain.

11. Repeat until all the doughnuts are made.

Tip: Want chocolate-covered doughnuts instead? Before frying the doughnuts, place 6 ounces (½ cup) of semisweet chips into a medium heat-resistant bowl. In a small microwave-safe bowl, heat 2 ounces (¼ cup) of heavy (whipping) cream in the microwave for about 1 minute. Pour the warm cream over the chocolate chips. Wait 1 minute and stir in 1 teaspoon of vanilla extract. Stir until all the chips are melted. Transfer the cooked doughnuts straight from the oil onto the cooling rack. Let cool a few minutes before placing them, one doughnut at a time, facedown into the chocolate. Swirl the chocolate a little and then carefully place the doughnuts back on the cooling rack, chocolate-side up.

Roasted Garlic and Cheddar Cheese Bialys

At first glance, a bialy looks like a bagel, as they are the same size and shape—but they are not the same. First of all, the hole in a bialy doesn't go all the way through. In that indention, there is usually some type of filling, such as onion or garlic. Nearly all bialy fillings are savory. Unlike bagels, bialys aren't boiled. They are baked, which helps make the bialy much softer and not as chewy. ***Makes 12 bialys***

FOR ACTIVATING THE STARTER

4¾ ounces (½ cup) sourdough starter

4 ounces (½ cup) lukewarm (90°F to 100°F) pure filtered or bottled water

4 ounces (1 cup) whole-wheat flour

FOR THE BIALY DOUGH

2.4 ounces (¼ cup) active sourdough starter

12 ounces (1½ cups) room temperature (75°F) pure filtered or bottled water

17 ounces (4 cups) unbleached all-purpose flour, unbleached bread flour, or whole-wheat flour, or a combination, plus more for dusting

1½ teaspoons fine sea salt

1 head garlic, roasted (see tip, page 48), cloves removed from their skins, mashed, and cooled

4 ounces (1 cup) grated extra-sharp white Cheddar cheese

PRE-PREP TIME: 6 TO 12 HOURS TO ACTIVATE THE STARTER
SUGGESTED STARTER: WHOLE WHEAT
SOURDOUGH METHOD: AMBIENT
PREP TIME: 9 HOURS 30 MINUTES
BAKING TIME: 12 MINUTES
TOTAL TIME: 9 HOURS 42 MINUTES

Tools needed
baking sheet

To activate the starter

At least 6 to 12 hours before making the dough, in a medium bowl, combine the starter, lukewarm water, and flour, completely incorporating the ingredients into the starter. Loosely cover and let sit on the counter until ready to use.

To make the bialy dough

1. In a large bowl, stir together the active starter and room temperature water until the starter completely dissolves into the water. Add the flour. Stir for as long as possible, then use your hands to get it to come together. Once the flour is incorporated, cover the bowl with a clean damp kitchen towel and let rest for 30 minutes.

2. Add the salt and, in the bowl, knead it in. Work the dough into a ball. Re-cover the bowl with the damp towel and let sit at room temperature overnight.

3. The next day, flour a breadboard or clean work surface and turn the dough out on to it. Press the dough into a log and shape. Cut the log into 12 even pieces. Roll each piece into a ball and sprinkle each ball with flour. Cover the balls with a clean kitchen towel and let them rest for 1 hour.

4. Preheat the oven to 450°F. Line a baking sheet with parchment paper.

5. Shape the balls into the size of a bagel, but without the hole. Working one at a time, dust the top of a bialy with flour and flip it over. Place it on the prepared baking sheet. Using 3 fingertips, make a deep indention in the top center of the bialy, but not so deep it goes all the way through. Stretch the indention a bit to widen the area. Repeat this with the remaining bialys.

6. Fill each of the indentions with roasted garlic and sprinkle the Cheddar cheese over the tops.

7. Bake for 10 to 12 minutes, or until the bialys are browned.

8. Transfer the bialys to a wire rack to cool. The bialys can be frozen to enjoy at a later time, if desired.

Tip: To save your Roasted Garlic and Cheddar Cheese Bialys to be eaten later, place them on a baking sheet and into the freezer overnight. The next day, transfer them to resealable freezer bags. These bialys will maintain their flavor for up to three months. Thaw in the refrigerator or place them directly on a lightly greased baking sheet. Heat at 350°F for 10 to 15 minutes until the cheese melts and the centers are warm.

Holiday Fruited Loaf

Enjoy this Holiday Fruited Loaf—don't worry, this isn't a fruitcake. This is a very tasty bread made with candied fruit. It's not a cake made with all fruit and little or no cake. It is very similar to a Norwegian bread called *julekake* and tastes best when lightly toasted and slathered with real butter. ***Makes 1 loaf***

FOR ACTIVATING THE STARTER

4¾ ounces (½ cup) sourdough starter

4 ounces (½ cup) lukewarm (90°F to 100°F) pure filtered or bottled water

4 ounces (scant 1 cup) unbleached all-purpose flour, or (1 cup) whole-wheat flour

FOR THE BREAD DOUGH

9½ ounces (2¼ cups) unbleached bread flour

1½ ounces (¼ cup) instant potato flakes

7 ounces (½ cup) sugar

2 teaspoons instant yeast, or bread machine yeast

1¼ teaspoons fine sea salt

½ teaspoon ground cardamom

6⅓ ounces (⅔ cup) active sourdough starter

6 ounces (¾ cup) lukewarm (90°F to 100°F) milk, plus more for coating the loaf (optional)

1 tablespoon butter, melted and cooled

1 pound (2 cups) mixed candied fruit

1¼ ounces (⅓ cup) old-fashioned rolled oats

Olive oil or nonstick cooking spray, for preparing the bowl and bread pan

PRE-PREP TIME: 6 TO 12 HOURS TO ACTIVATE THE STARTER

SUGGESTED STARTER: UNBLEACHED ALL-PURPOSE OR WHOLE WHEAT

SOURDOUGH METHOD: AMBIENT

PREP TIME: 2 HOURS 30 MINUTES

BAKING TIME: 45 MINUTES

TOTAL TIME: 3 HOURS 15 MINUTES

Tools needed

8½-by-4½-inch bread pan, stand mixer or handheld electric mixer

To activate the starter

At least 6 to 12 hours before making the dough, in a medium bowl, combine the starter, lukewarm water, and flour, completely incorporating the ingredients into the starter. Loosely cover and let sit on the counter until ready to use.

To make the bread dough

1. In a large bowl, whisk the flour, potato flakes, sugar, yeast, salt, and cardamom until combined. Set aside.

2. In the bowl of a stand mixer fitted with the dough hook, or in another large bowl and using a handheld electric mixer, mix the active starter, milk, and butter on low speed until combined.

3. Add the flour mixture to the sourdough mixture. Mix on low speed (you may have to use a sturdy spoon or spatula if mixing by hand) until combined. When the dough becomes too stiff, use your hands to knead it.

4. Add the candied fruit and oats. By hand, in the bowl (or turn it out onto a floured surface), knead them in until combined. Shape the dough into a ball.

5. Coat another large bowl with olive oil and transfer the dough to it, turning to coat all sides. Cover with a clean kitchen towel and let rise for 90 minutes.

6. Lightly coat an 8½-by-4½-inch bread pan with cooking spray and set aside.

7. Flour a breadboard or clean work surface and turn the dough out on to it. Shape the dough into a rectangle no wider than the prepared bread pan. Roll up the rectangle from one short side and place the dough, seam-side down, into the prepared pan. Re-cover the dough and let the bread rise for another hour.

8. Preheat the oven to 350°F.

9. For a shiny crust, if you like, use a pastry brush to paint the top of the loaf with milk.

10. Bake the bread for 40 to 45 minutes, or until it reaches an internal temperature of 200°F on a digital food thermometer.

11. Transfer the bread to a wire rack to cool in the pan for 5 minutes. Remove the bread from the pan and place it on the wire rack to cool completely before slicing into it.

Tip: Mixed candied fruit has cherries, pineapple, lemon peel, orange peel, and citron. You don't have to use the mixed variety, though; you can just use candied cherries or pineapple. Using red and green cherries offers more of a holiday vibe. Candied pineapple is pretty, too. If the pieces seem too big, cut them. To keep the fruit from sticking to your knife, wet the knife first. Continue to wet the knife as needed.

GLOSSARY

active sourdough starter: Sourdough starter fed within the last 6 to 12 hours

active yeast: A type of yeast that must be dried and proofed in warm (100°F to 125°F) water before using

ambient: The temperature when dough is proofed at room or warm temperature

autolyze: The (about) 20-minute rest time for dough after mixing the sourdough starter with flour and water, but before the salt is added

baguette: A hand-shaped long, skinny loaf

baker's percentage: A method used to formulate a recipe without having all the specific measurements, and when flour is calculated at 100 percent; the remaining calculations are figured from there; only used with recipes when ingredients are measured in grams

baking stone: A clay surface, placed in a cold oven, that heats up as the oven heats and provides an even surface to bake breads or pizzas, producing crunchy bottom crusts

banneton: A wicker basket that makes a circular pattern in the dough while it's proofing in it

barm: Another name for a wet sourdough starter, but with no additional yeast added

batard: An oval bread shape about one-third the length of a baguette

benching: The resting time after the dough is divided but before baking

biga: Italian version of a sourdough starter to which, besides the flour and water, dry yeast is added to boost the wild yeast found in the flour

bloom (blooming): Another word for activate. Warm (100°F to 125°F) water is needed to bloom, or activate, dry yeast.

boule: Round bread loaf that is great for serving soups and dips in when it's hollowed out.

bread lame (a.k.a. lame): A very sharp utensil, typically made with a razor blade, used to slash the top of a loaf of sourdough bread

bread machine yeast: Typically sold in jars; does not have to be dissolved in water before using

brotform: German version of a banneton proofing basket (*see* banneton)

bulk ferment: When bread dough is allowed to proof one last time before dividing it into multiple loaves

chef: One of many names for sourdough starter

cool water: Water whose temperature is between 60°F and 70°F

couche: A cloth used to support the already-shaped bread dough as it rises one more time before baking

crumb: The inside, or texture, of a sourdough, which is desired as soft and full of large holes

discard: The part of the sourdough starter often discarded during the feeding process

dock (docking): The process of making indentations in bread dough, or poking holes into the bottom of an unfilled, unbaked piecrust, before baking to keep it from bubbling up during baking

dough: The product of mixing flour with other ingredients to make a loaf of bread or a piecrust

elasticity: After kneading, the dough's ability to bounce back after being pressed with a finger

feeding: The addition of a consistent amount of water and flour to the starter on a consistent schedule

folding: The best way to knead a particularly sticky dough without adding extra flour, similar to making an envelope out of a piece of paper: On a flat round or oval piece of dough, stretch and fold down the top to just past the middle; turn the dough and repeat until the dough has had a complete 360-degree turn, and again until the dough becomes manageable and less sticky.

fresh starter: The same as an active starter, having been fed and ready to use

gluten: A mixture of two proteins that makes bread dough elastic

hooch: The liquid that forms on the top of the sourdough starter after it has sat for a day or two, and that is stirred back into it

instant yeast: Yeast dried and ground into a fine powder that doesn't need to be proofed before using

knead: Using your hands to incorporate ingredients into the bread dough and also to work, stretch, form, or shape it

levain: The French word for sourdough starter; a pre-fermented *levain* is made by adding dry yeast to the starter

lukewarm: The temperature between room temperature and warm— from 90°F to 100°F

mother: Another name for sourdough starter

oven spring: A sudden, quick rise of the bread immediately after being put into the oven

resting: That period of time between mixing and kneading dough

pizza peel: A handy tool made of wood or stainless steel with a long handle and a large rounded end that squares up toward the handle's end; especially important to have if baking stones are used

poolish: A Polish term coined in reference to their version of a high hydration sourdough starter

pre-ferment: To add dry yeast to a wild yeast sourdough starter

proof (proofing): Letting bread dough rest to double in size

reactivation: The process to reviving sourdough starter from a dried state

retarded bread: Bread placed in the refrigerator to slow its final rising

ripe starter: Starter that has been fed and that is ready for making bread

room temperature: As far as bread proofing and rising go, around 75°F

score (a.k.a. slash): Using a bread lame or very sharp knife to slash into the bread dough to control the area of the rising dough

sourdough: Sour dough made by making a sourdough starter, which is made by combining flour and water that, over time, becomes sour from sitting out

sponge: Another name for sourdough starter that may or may not have any additional yeast

starter: Sourdough starter, a.k.a. starter; the fermented version of flour and water

stretch and fold: A way of kneading wet dough (*see* folding)

warm water: Water whose temperature is between 100°F and 125°F

wild yeast: Yeast that is found everywhere, including in the air and in the flour, which is why no additional yeast is necessary to make a good sourdough starter

Different Sourdough Cultures and Flavor Profiles Around the World

Want to experience different tastes and textures of sourdough starters from around the world? Due to varying climates and terrain, they can be quite different. Here are several sourdough starters that can be bought online.

NAME AND/OR LOCATION OF SOURDOUGH STARTER	TYPE OF FLOUR USED	FLAVOR PROFILE
Alaskan	White	This starter will proof quickly; good with any baked goods
Australian Tasmanian Devil	Wheat	Distinct flavor; works best with kamut and spelt flours
Austrian Rye	Rye	Rye flour is itself already sour; sourness peaks in this starter
Belgium Desem	Whole wheat	Longer proofing; more in-depth sour flavor
Egyptian Giza	Whole wheat	All-purpose starter; works best with pitas and naans
Finland	Wheat	A good riser; best for hearty breads and sourdough crackers
Italian Camaldoli	White	Use in pizzas, ciabattas, and country breads; easy to maintain
Italian Ischia	White	For those connoisseurs who prefer a sourer bread; use with most breads
New England	White	Quick riser with an all-around flavor; good for all baked goods
New England Brown Rice	Brown rice	A gluten-free alternative; needs to be fed often
New England Spelt	Spelt	Nutty, slightly sweet flavor shines through; good for sandwich breads and rolls
Parisian	White	Not overly sour; works well with all artisanal breads
Polish	Rye	Robust culture; works best with pumpernickel and other rye flours
San Francisco	White	One to mimic; used mostly in a boule

MEASUREMENTS AND CONVERSION TABLES

VOLUME EQUIVALENTS (LIQUID)

US STANDARD	US STANDARD (OUNCES)	METRIC (APPROXIMATE)
2 tablespoons	1 fl. oz.	30 mL
¼ cup	2 fl. oz.	60 mL
½ cup	4 fl. oz.	120 mL
1 cup	8 fl. oz.	240 mL
1 ½ cups	12 fl. oz.	355 mL
2 cups or 1 pint	16 fl. oz.	475 mL
4 cups or 1 quart	32 fl. oz.	1 L
1 gallon	128 fl. oz.	4 L

OVEN TEMPERATURES

FAHRENHEIT (F)	CELSIUS (C) (APPROXIMATE)
250°	120°
300°	150°
325°	165°
350°	180°
375°	190°
400°	200°
425°	220°
450°	230°

VOLUME EQUIVALENTS (DRY)

US STANDARD	METRIC (APPROXIMATE)
⅛ teaspoon	0.5 mL
¼ teaspoon	1 mL
½ teaspoon	2 mL
¾ teaspoon	4 mL
1 teaspoon	5 mL
1 tablespoon	15 mL
¼ cup	59 mL
⅓ cup	79 mL
½ cup	118 mL
⅔ cup	156 mL
¾ cup	177 mL
1 cup	235 mL
2 cups or 1 pint	475 mL
3 cups	700 mL
4 cups or 1 quart	1 L

WEIGHT EQUIVALENTS

US STANDARD	METRIC (APPROXIMATE)
½ ounce	15 g
1 ounce	30 g
2 ounces	60 g
4 ounces	115 g
8 ounces	225 g
12 ounces	340 g
16 ounces or 1 pound	455 g

RECIPE INDEX

INDEX

ACKNOWLEDGMENTS

A special thanks to Aileen and Arlene for tirelessly reading over my pages.

Thanks to Debby, my favorite author and friend, who helped me understand all things in writing and book publishing.

ABOUT THE AUTHOR

Carroll Pellegrinelli has been baking for as long as she can remember. Under her mother's guidance she began creaming her butter and sugars as soon as she could reach the counter. A few years later, in a self-preservation effort, her father took up bread baking. He found that kneading dough alleviates work-related stress. Carroll soon followed suit and began baking bread, too. For almost 20 years Carroll wrote about desserts and baking for About.com, which was owned by the *New York Times*. Combining her love of food and travel, Carroll wrote the first book in a series of adventure travel cookbooks: *Travel with the Lee Girls, As They Shop and Eat Their Way Through the South, New Orleans and the French Quarter*. The book is available on Amazon in paperback and as an e-book.